III

Though thou sing my forebears praises
With inspired minstrelsy,
And innumerate their phases
Of incipient Lunacy,

IV

Thou dost wish, (and well I know it)
Weaned of the Castalian spring
Me, an unexpected poet,
Hectic rhapsodies to sing.

BLOOMSBURY STUD

THE LIFE OF
STEPHEN 'TOMMY' TOMLIN

to Harold

BLOOMSBURY STUD

THE LIFE OF
STEPHEN 'TOMMY' TOMLIN

from

Michael Bloch & Susan Fox

Michael

24 ix 20

M·A·B
MMXX

First published in 2020 by
M.A.B.
2 Strathearn Place, London W2 2NQ

www.bloomsburystud.net

This first edition comprises 600 copies

Text © Michael Bloch and Susan Fox, 2020
Images © as stated in the List of Illustrations

The moral right of Michael Bloch and Susan Fox to be identified as the
authors of this work has been asserted in accordance with the
Copyright, Designs and Patents Act, 1988

ISBN: 978-1-9163254-0-1

A catalogue record for this book is available
from the British Library

Designed in Adobe Caslon by Libanus Press Ltd, Marlborough
and printed in the UK by Gomer Press

CONTENTS

LIST OF ILLUSTRATIONS

King's photograph collections of Lytton Strachey, Dora Carrington and
     Frances Partridge at King's College, Cambridge
NPG National Portrait Gallery, London
Tate photograph albums of John Banting and Barbara Ker-Seymer in
     Tate Gallery Archives, London

To Norman Coates

INTRODUCTION &
ACKNOWLEDGEMENTS

It is said that the most brilliant, brave and beautiful Englishmen die young. In his *The Fatal Englishman* (1996) Sebastian Faulks vividly describes three such men who lived during the first half of the twentieth century – the painter Christopher Wood, who threw himself under a train, aged twenty-nine; the aviator Richard Hillary, who embarked on a suicidal flying mission, aged twenty-three; and the journalist Jeremy Wolfenden, who drowned mysteriously in his bath, aged thirty-one.

To these names might be added that of the sculptor Stephen Tomlin (1901–37), who was born a month before Wood, dazzled his contemporaries (including many of the great and famous) with his talent and personality, and died aged thirty-five ostensibly as the result of an infection following a tooth extraction – though his intimates had little doubt that the underlying cause of his demise was the heavy drinking (compounded by drug-taking) to which (like Wolfenden) he had increasingly abandoned himself during the last years of his short and turbulent life.

'Tommy' (as he was known to his friends) was a man of many gifts. He was a fine sculptor, known particularly for his portrait heads, examples of which may be seen in the National Portrait Gallery, Tate Britain, and the Bloomsbury shrine at Charleston in East Sussex. But he also distinguished himself as a poet, an actor, a musician, a ceramicist and a stage designer, in any of which fields he might have achieved fame. Like his Oxford contemporary and intimate friend

Roy Harrod, he also had the potential to make a brilliant academic career – though such a future held no interest for him, and he abandoned the university after only two terms.

He was also (according to many of those who knew him) a fascinating talker, possessed of a beautiful voice and a quick, incisive mind; and he radiated sex-appeal and charm. These attributes won him the admiration of the Bloomsbury Group, to which he was introduced by the novelist David Garnett at the age of twenty-two: within a short time he was on terms of close friendship with many of its leading figures, including Duncan Grant, Lytton Strachey (whose niece he married), Dora Carrington and John Maynard Keynes. Only Virginia Woolf proved resistant to his attractions – though ironically he is probably now best known for the bust of her (copies of which may be seen at her country house in Sussex and near the site of her London house in Tavistock Square, as well as at the British Library, the NPG and Charleston) which he sculpted in 1931.

Moreover, Tommy – who, in addition to his wonderful voice and famous charm, possessed (from adolescence up to his late twenties) an alluring appearance and a splendid muscular physique – was a renowned and compulsive seducer. He was bisexual; he bowled over most of those he met; and, if he found them in any way attractive or interesting, he aspired to make love to them, irrespective of their age or sex. As his much-suffering wife Julia wrote: 'Tommy's daemon insisted that not only with their souls but also with their *bodies* everyone must him worship.' Although we have few details of his affairs (if one can so describe his innumerable sexual encounters), sufficient testimony survives to make us aware that he was a legend in his lifetime for his erotomania and the scale and variety of his conquests.

Tommy's biography is a challenging undertaking – like trying to complete a jigsaw puzzle with most of the pieces missing. He left few papers; and as well as not keeping letters he did not like writing them – such of his missives as have been preserved by their recipients, though penned in an artistic hand, and elegantly phrased, tend to be

brief and uninformative. Indeed, he was by nature elusive and mysterious, even his close friends often having little idea where he was or
what he was up to. Behind his many talents and attractions lay a very
dark psychology, including a strain of sinister malevolence – though
a comprehensive view of the influences which may have been responsible for the demonic side of his nature was probably vouchsafed only
to the psychoanalysts he consulted during his adult life.

Yet considerable, if fragmentary, evidence about him exists in the
form of the letters, diaries and memoirs of those who knew him,
were fascinated by him, and in many cases loved him. And with his
arresting looks, he was much drawn, painted and photographed.

Susan Fox is a professional researcher; Michael Bloch is a professional writer. Together we have tried to bring into focus this unusual,
brilliant and disturbed figure. The portrait is inevitably far from
complete; and many questions arise to which one can only guess the
answers. We nevertheless feel the quest has been worthwhile; and
perhaps the appearance of this biography will prompt the disclosure
of further material which may dispel some of the mystery.

In acknowledging the help we received, two debts must be mentioned
particularly. Philip Trower, born in 1924, was Tommy's nephew,
younger son of his elder sister Joan. A fund of family information, he
was the only person we encountered who knew Tommy, a favourite
uncle whose company he enjoyed and whose memory he cherished.
He retained a sparkling intelligence up to his death in January 2019,
and was generous with his help and patient with our enquiries.
Oliver Garnett is the grandson of Tommy's great friend David
'Bunny' Garnett. As a Cambridge art history undergraduate in the
late 1970s he wrote a dissertation entitled *The Sculpture of Stephen
Tomlin*, which (so far as we are aware) is the only monograph so far
to have been written on the subject of Tommy. (It has never been
published, but a copy may be consulted in the Tate Gallery archives.)
Not only has this work been of great help to us, but he too has been

generous in responding to our enquiries, and in sharing with us the documents he collected, the photographs he took of Tommy's sculpture, and the notes of interviews he secured with persons who had known Tommy when he worked on his dissertation forty years ago.

We are also grateful to following for assisting us in various ways: Philip Athill; Elinor Bagenal; Benjamin Bather; Christopher Bellew; Julian Berkeley; Emily Bingham; David Bonner; Tony Bradshaw; Nicola Browne; Billie Buckley; Stephen Carroll; Eva Chadwick; Anne Chisholm; Richard Davenport Hines; Patric Dickinson; Hannah Dunn; Tom Edwards; Peter Ewart; Francis Ford; Michael Fox; Harriet Frazer; Simon Frazer; Henrietta Garnett; Jane Garnett; Richard Garnett; Adrian Gibbs; Martin Gibson; Nicholas Goddard; Libby Goldby; Roger Goldby; Stephen Goldby; Robert Harding; Henry Harrod; Selina Hastings; Alan Hawley; David Herbert; Martin Huber; Jeffrey Isaacs; Stephen Keynes; Sarah Knights; Neil McKenna; Philip Mansel; Robbie Macdonald; Ursula Mackenzie; Lord Marks of Broughton (Simon Marks); Caroline Moorhead; Alastair Morrison; Lord Moyne (Jonathan Guinness); Rosaleen Mulji; Charles Orwin; Frances Partridge; Roger Peers; Charlotte Philipps; Paul Quarrie; Donald Rice; Jon Richardson; Ray Roberts; Jans Ondaatje Rolls; Tony Scotland; Carmen Königsreuther Socknat; Steve Tatti; Gini Trower; Jonathan Trower; William Trower; Oliver White; Susan Wightman and Ed Wilson.

We have been supplied with research material by the archives of the following institutions (the names of those who assisted us in brackets): Archives New Zealand (Alice Meads); Berg Collection, New York Public Library (Stephen Crook); British Library; Boston College, John J. Burns Library (Shelley Barber); Christ Church Art Gallery, New Zealand (Tim Jones); Dorset County Museum, Dorchester (Anna Butler and Carol Graham); Eton College Library (Sally Jennings); Harrow School (Joanna Badrock); Houghton Library, Harvard University; Henry Moore Institute (Claire Mayoh); King's College, Cambridge (Patricia McGuire); Library of Congress; Lincoln's

Inn, London (Dunstan Speight); Museum of London (Beverley Cook); National Portrait Gallery, London (Emma Butterfield); New College, Oxford (Jennifer Thorp); Northwestern University Libraries (Nick Munagian); Powys Society; Tate Gallery; University College London Special Collections (Mandy Wise); University of Sussex Special Collections (Rose Lock); University of Texas at Austin, Harry Ransom Center (Jean Cannon); University of Tulsa, McFarlin Library (Jennifer Murphy); Wiltshire Record Office, Chippenham.

Although Tommy was estranged from his wife Julia during his last years (to the point that he did not wish to see her when she attempted to visit him on his deathbed), they never divorced; and as he died intestate, she inherited his estate, including the copyright in both his writing and his artistic work. By her will dated 6 January 1971, Julia, who died in 1979, bequeathed all copyrights in her ownership to her friend, the British art historian John Russell. The copyright of both Tommy and Julia is now owned by Russell's daughter Lavinia, married to the architect Sir Nicholas Grimshaw. We are grateful to Lady Grimshaw for generously granting us permission to quote the words of Tommy and Julia, and to reproduce images of Tommy's sculpture. Others to whom we are indebted for permission to quote words or reproduce images are Primrose Campbell (Henry Lamb); Gill Coleridge and Sophie Partridge (Dora Carrington and Frances Partridge); Henrietta Garnett (Vanessa Bell); Oliver Garnett (David Garnett, and his own photographs); Max Ker-Seymer (Barbara Ker-Seymer); Alicia Ofori of Random House (Virginia Woolf); Lisa Olrichs (NPG images); Jacqueline Simon of the Artists Rights Society (Duncan Grant); David Thompson (Tate Gallery images); and Allan Warren (his photographs of the authors). If there are any rights we have failed to acknowledge we will endeavour to correct the omission in future editions.

Last but not least we thank our friend Norman Coates, who owns John Banting's splendid portrait of Tommy which adorns the cover, and to whom the book is dedicated.

Tommy towards the end of his Harrow schooldays

I

EARLY YEARS

1901–1921

Stephen 'Tommy' Tomlin was born on 2 March 1901 – six weeks after the death of Queen Victoria – at 5 Clifton Place, a large stuccoed terrace house in the London Borough of Paddington, a few minutes' walk from Hyde Park and Paddington Station.

His father, Thomas James Chesshyre Tomlin (1867–1935), was a successful Chancery barrister, brilliant and dry, who would go on to become a distinguished King's Counsel and high court judge, reaching the pinnacle of his profession when he was appointed a law lord in 1929 as Baron Tomlin of Ash in the County of Kent.

The Tomlins are an old Kentish gentry family, said to descend from the barber of King Edward III. From the late middle ages they were landowners in Thanet; the parish church of Ash, an ancient village situated midway between Canterbury and Sandwich, is filled with their graves and memorials. Tommy's grandfather, George Tomlin of Ash, was also a barrister, married to the daughter of an eminent clergyman, Canon Chesshyre of Canterbury; but he died young, and his son Thomas worked hard to establish himself in the profession and support his mother and sisters. Thomas married Marion Waterfield, whose father, Colonel Garrow Waterfield, had governed the wild North-West Frontier of British India. Marion's mother, *née* Clarke, was the granddaughter of a royal physician, Sir Charles Mansfield Clarke, who had been created a baronet in 1831 by King William IV; Marion's uncle, the 3rd Baronet, was a distinguished soldier who had seen active service from the Crimean War to the Boer War, and held the post of Quartermaster-General of the British Army at the time of Tommy's birth.[1]

Tommy's family background, therefore, was filled with high-achievers in the realms of imperial administration, the Army, the Church, medicine and the law. In his short, brilliant and tempestuous life he would rebel against these generations of respectable, dutiful men and the world they represented.

Tommy was the fourth of five children. The eldest, Joan, was a strong-willed girl of whom they were all in awe. There followed three boys: as the eldest, Anthony, suffered from indifferent health, and the second, Garrow, was not academically inclined, there was an onus on Tommy, the youngest son, to shine and succeed. Helen, the baby of the family, was born five years after Tommy; until she married in 1932 and went to live overseas, she and Tommy were united by a close bond. Tommy, who was noticeably shorter than his siblings, received the nickname 'Tom-Tit' – hence 'Tommy', the name by which he would be known by friends and relations throughout his life.

We know little of Tommy's childhood except that, although physically robust, he was given to melancholy moods. He told Virginia Woolf that his psychological 'sufferings' largely arose from the fact that, as a child, he had been 'misunderstood' by his parents.[2] His father was a somewhat austere figure of whom his children saw little owing to his immersion in his professional work; his mother (caricatured by Tommy's future wife Julia as Mrs Thatcham in her novel *Cheerful Weather for the Wedding*) was a conventional and rather imperious matron who tended to deal with life's problems by ignoring them. Like many offspring of upper-middle-class Edwardian families, the Tomlin children tended to receive more affection from the servants at Clifton Place – 'Meela' the cook, Stewart the parlourmaid and Yvonne the French nurse-maid – than from their parents.[3] Once, when Tommy was staying with a cousin, a childless lady living in a large house, he was found sitting at the bottom of the stairs with his head in his hands, repeating to himself: 'She doesn't understand children! She doesn't understand children!'[4]

But he seems to have enjoyed his holidays, generally spent with his siblings in Kent. Sometimes they stayed with their Tomlin grandmother, an eccentric Victorian recluse, swathed in black, who lived at the Red House near Ash, looked after by a succession of boys from the village whom she called her 'Boots', who became playmates of the Tomlin children.[5] At other times they stayed at Upper Hardres Manor south of Canterbury with their father's sister, Aunt Bessie, childlessly married to a gentleman of leisure, William Lochée: set in an area of glorious wooded downland later rhapsodised in the novels of Jocelyn Brooke,[6] Upper Hardres was a paradise to which Tommy retreated at stressful moments of his adult life.

Early Victorian architecture in Clifton Place: the house in which Tommy was born and brought up was eventually demolished and replaced by a modern block of flats, but part of the original terrace survives at the end of the street

Marion Tomlin holding the infant Tommy, with her three eldest children
(left to right) Anthony, Joan and Garrow

Although neither of Tommy's parents seems to have had a highly
developed aesthetic sense, there were artists in the family. Another
of his father's sisters was married to an Italian painter (known
for historical conversation pieces) named Sabatini. A cousin of his
mother, Aubrey Waterfield (1874–1944), who lived in a castle in Italy,
was a talented portraitist and watercolourist (said by Kenneth
Clark to be the most gifted English artist of his time who was not
well-known to the public).

Another relation of whom Tommy would have seen something
during his formative years was his mother's elder brother, Neville
Waterfield (1864–1940). From 1890 to 1903, Neville was private
secretary to the Liberal grandee Lord Rosebery, who served as

Tommy as a small child

Prime Minister for fifteen months in 1894–5. A widower rumoured to possess homosexual inclinations, Rosebery surrounded himself with handsome male secretaries, and Neville, whom he treated like a son,* was one of the handsomest: staying with Rosebery in 1898, Raymond Asquith wrote to his father Herbert (the future Liberal premier) that Waterfield with his striking looks 'inclines one to believe the worst of his illustrious master'.[7] On leaving Rosebery's

---

* In his biography of Rosebery, his son-in-law Lord Crewe wrote that 'Rosebery depended much on the friendship and service of his personal private secretary Neville Waterfield, his perpetual companion and the recipient of greater confidence than as a rule he felt able to give his nearest belongings'. (The Marquess of Crewe, *Lord Rosebery* [1931], Vol. II, p. 633.)

Tommy (top right) in his house football team at Harrow, 1918

service Neville spent the rest of his career as secretary to the Oxford University Appointments Committee, marrying in 1922 at the age of fifty-seven.

Tommy's father had been a brilliant pupil at Harrow, where he was Head of School in 1890, and had gone on to distinguish himself academically at New College, Oxford; and Tommy was expected to follow in his footsteps. After attending Copthorne, a preparatory school in Sussex, he entered Harrow as a Foundation Scholar in September 1914. His housemaster was N. K. Stephen, an easygoing bachelor who ran his house with his sister. During the thirteen terms he spent there Tommy distinguished himself in various ways. He excelled in examinations. He won prizes for Latin, reading and poetry. He became one of the 'School Twelve' – Harrow's top singers. He was a leading light of school music-making, debating and dramatics. He was a member of his house football team, and appointed a monitor (a house prefect). His

achievements were often mentioned in the official school maga-
zine *The Harrovian*.[8] His poem *Jerusalem*, awarded the school poetry
prize at the end of 1917, not only shows literary talent but suggests
an interest in current affairs: a rollicking pastiche of rhyming
couplets in the style of Byron, it compares the city at the height
of its glory under Solomon, the depths of its depravity under the
Kings of Judah and at the time of Jesus, ending with a reference to
the desire of the Jews (just enshrined in the Balfour Declaration of
November 1917) to make it the capital of their national homeland.[9]

Tommy was popular with his contemporaries and formed
enduring friendships with several other boys, including Angus
Davidson (a future publisher and translator) and his brother
Douglas (a future artist and illustrator), George Howe (a future
actor), and Gerald Gardiner (a future barrister who would become
Lord Chancellor in the 1960s Labour Government). Though he
remained rather short,* he had an engaging appearance, a seductive
voice, and a splendid muscular physique; and some of these friendships contained a romantic (and almost certainly sexual) element:
Angus Davidson conceived a passionate (and intermittently reciprocated) 'crush' on Tommy which continued long after they had
left the school. Indeed, although sexual frolics had to be conducted
in the greatest secrecy, and exposure generally meant expulsion,
Harrow had something of a reputation as the most 'homosexual'
of the leading public schools.† Tommy also befriended Sylvia
Townsend Warner, daughter of Harrow's history master and later
famous as a novelist: she was seven years older than Tommy.
Although Sylvia went to work in a munitions factory in 1915, and
her father died in 1916, she maintained her connection with Harrow

---

* Five feet six inches in adult life.
† As a pupil in the 1850s, John Addington Symonds had been shocked to discover
that almost every senior boy had his 'bitch' (a junior boy for his sexual gratification);
and three-quarters of a century later a recent pupil, the sociologist Tom Harrison,
could still write that 'when you say Harrow you say perversion' (quoted in Judith M.
Heimann, *The Most Offending Soul Alive* [1997], pp.13–14).

through her close friendship (they were in fact secret lovers) with the Harrow music master Dr Percy Buck, who in 1917 obtained for her the job of editing a collection of early church music. Tommy, as one of the top school singers, was a favourite pupil of Buck, and during his school years the wise and sympathetic Sylvia became something of a mother figure, to whom he frequently turned for comfort and advice.[10] (She later wrote that, at school, Tommy 'was popular, successful and unhappy', whereas at home he was 'merely unhappy'.[11])

Gerald Gardiner (whom Tommy got to know well, as his family lived at Hardres Court in Kent, the neighbouring estate to Upper Hardres Manor where Tommy spent his holidays) later claimed that the Harrow master who most influenced him was the Reverend D. R. Kittermaster (1877–1965), a classicist who was engaged shortly before the First World War, received an MC for his exploits on the Western Front, and (having been invalided out of the Army) returned to the school to run the cadet force as well as to teach Latin. As a young clergyman Kittermaster had worked in borstals and prisons, and he showed particular interest in unusual or rebellious boys, who were known as 'Kitter's criminals'. He made no secret of his left-wing views, and put Gardiner on the path to becoming a socialist. It is probable that he also exercised a strong influence on Tommy.[12]

Tommy's father doubtless hoped that Tommy would emulate him by becoming Head of School; but in Tommy's last term, in the autumn of 1918, the position went to another good-looking and brilliant boy, Rupert Buxton. Tommy and Buxton seem to have been friendly rivals. Both had a touch of melancholy about them. They were among the leading school poets. When the school debating society discussed the motion 'that the Public Schools do not satisfy the needs of the Nation', it was proposed by Tommy (supported by Dr Buck) and opposed by Buxton. (Though the motion was defeated, *The Harrovian* thought Tommy's the better spcech.) And when the school's Shakespeare Society mounted a production of *Twelfth Night*, Tommy, playing Malvolio, was agreed to be the star, eclipsing Buxton's Andrew Aguecheek.[13] Then, in December 1918, a few days before the end of term, a bizarre event occurred. Buxton suddenly vanished, having announced that he had received a letter requesting his help. No one knew where he had gone. A few days later he sent a telegram confirming that he was safe in Newcastle. The episode (which featured in the national press) was never explained; it was assumed that Buxton had suffered a mental breakdown, and he did not return to the school.

Tommy too seems to have been in a state of mental turmoil towards the end of his school career. This is perhaps not surprising – for he arrived at Harrow in September 1914, the month after the outbreak of the First World War, and left in December 1918, the month after its conclusion. Month after month, term after term, he endured the trauma of seeing boys not much older than himself, some of whom he had loved or admired, leave for the war, and

ABOVE: Rupert Buxton

LEFT: Sylvia Townsend Warner

either not return at all, or do so horribly mutilated in body or mind.* But in Tommy's case there was an additional trauma. His eldest brother Anthony, born in 1895, had preceded him at Harrow, and in 1913 went on (like their father) to New College, Oxford. When war broke out he did not volunteer for the Army, but remained at Oxford; and when, in March 1916, compulsory military service was introduced in England, he sailed (accompanied by his sister Joan) for New Zealand, where he worked as tutor to the children of a landowner near Christchurch. In December 1917 he died there – soon after his name had appeared on a list of men in the Christchurch district who were due to be called up for service in Europe.[14] His death certificate, signed by his doctor, states that he died of heart failure caused by myocarditis (though he had been in reasonable health during recent weeks, riding his horse at a local agricultural show). It was said that Anthony, owing to his heart condition, had been unfit for service, but suffered humiliation in England owing to his deceptively healthy appearance, hence his departure for the Antipodes. Whatever the truth of the matter, Anthony's fate must have caused intense pain and some embarrassment to his family, and especially his two younger brothers. (The middle brother, Garrow, born in 1898, survived gallant service in the Royal Navy, in motor torpedo boats.)

That the end of hostilites left Tommy with a sense of desolation is suggested by a sonnet he wrote at the time of the Armistice:

> Now every poet sings of Peace; but I
> ... dare not sing of Peace while Empires die
> And earth is royal with the blood of Kings,
> And nations clog the Gates of Liberty,
> And men are dazed by half-conceivéd things.
> No mortal one has any song for this ...[15]

---

* 2,917 Harrovians served in the war, of whom 609 were wounded and 644 were killed – not counting those who died later of their wounds.

Meanwhile, aged just seventeen, Tommy had won an exhibition to New College, and he arrived there to read history in January 1919. (The college's Warden was W. A. Spooner, famous for his verbal slips; and the history tutor, then on leave serving as Lloyd George's education minister, was H. A. L. Fisher, a cousin of Virginia Woolf and a sometime fellow student of Tommy's father.) There again, he found himself haunted by the ghosts of the recently dead: no fewer than 228 members and staff of the college had fallen in the Great War. He was no doubt haunted too by the tragic memory of Anthony, who had been obliged to abandon his studies there less than three years earlier. Moreover, during the war the college had doubled as a military hospital, and in the winter of Tommy's arrival its quadrangles were still full of tents housing wounded soldiers. From the moment he arrived there, Tommy seems to have been miserably unhappy.* On the other hand, he was morbidly fascinated by the Shelley Memorial[16] – an enormous homoerotic recumbent nude statue of the drowned poet, by the Victorian sculptor Henry Onslow Ford, which nearby University College had accepted from the Shelley family in 1893 (with some misgivings, not only on account of its sexually suggestive nature but also because Shelley had been expelled from that college for his atheistic views): Tommy (we are told) would stare at it for hours.

At Oxford Tommy continued to see something of Sylvia, who regularly visited the Bodleian Library in connection with her research on music manuscripts. He confided to her that he hated Oxford; that he felt oppressed by its architecture; and that, although his mentors assured him that he could have a brilliant academic career if he put his mind to it, he longed to give it up to become 'an artisan'. One day towards the end of Tommy's first term, Sylvia

* In the autumn of 1924, when depressed owing to his unhappy love affair with Henrietta Bingham (described in Chapter 3), Tommy wrote to Carrington that 'I have not had such an attack since I was 17' (Carrington Papers, British Library).

was visited in London by Tommy's mother, who explained that she and her husband were 'desperately anxious' about their son, who had vanished from Oxford two days earlier without telling anyone where he was going. Sylvia regretted that she had no idea where he might be; but while they were talking she received a telegram from Tommy asking her to write to him at an inn in Cornwall, the Tinner's Arms at Zennor. Mrs Tomlin was relieved to know of her son's whereabouts, but confided that 'he's a great disappointment to his father'.[17] (Thomas Tomlin's disappointment must have been particularly acute as Tommy had been the academic star among his three sons – though Garrow was not stupid, and after his discharge from the navy was admitted to Magdalene College, Cambridge to read engineering. He was however pleased when, in September 1920, his formidable daughter Joan, who during the war had worked as a VAD nurse, married William 'Tom' Trower, a prosperous solicitor from whose firm Thomas received much of his lucrative work at the bar, and whose family owned a beautiful estate in Hertfordshire.)

At their meeting of 23 March 1919, the Warden and Tutors of New College reprimanded Tommy for going absent without leave, together with a fellow undergraduate named Stirling. However, less than three months later he again disappeared before the end of term, this time with an undergraduate named Braybrooke. It was almost as if he sought to emulate the escapade of Rupert Buxton at Harrow, mysteriously vanishing as a prelude to 'dropping out'. Moreover, Tommy, who just a few months earlier had sailed through Responsions (an examination needed to enter the university), managed to fail his preliminary history exams that June, suggesting that he had done no work. It was probably on account of his father's influence that Tommy was not summarily expelled at that point, for in the autumn of 1919 he was still registered as an undergraduate member of the college, though described as 'non-resident'. Possibly he continued to attend lectures and tutorials for a time; but the authorities soon concluded (as his New College contemporary Maurice Bowra, later a famous don, puts it in his memoirs[*]) that Tommy 'believed neither in himself nor in Oxford'. After 1919, his name vanishes from the register.[18] (When asked what had become of him, Warden Spooner, in something of a 'spoonerism', declared: 'Mr Tomlin will not recur.')[19]

Tommy seems to have made only one friend at Oxford to whom he subsequently remained close. This was Roy Harrod (1900–78), who was one year older but arrived at New College at the same time, having briefly served in the army towards the end of the war. Letters from Tommy among Harrod's papers[20] (along with the poem dedicated to Harrod quoted below) leave little doubt that they had a gay affair, which began at Oxford and continued intermittently thereafter. (In a letter sent after Tommy's death to his widow Julia, Harrod wrote that Tommy was 'the biggest influence

Roy Harrod

* Bowra mentions that he and Tommy were among four New College undergraduates who possessed a remarkable ability to express themselves in verse, the others being the Scottish aristocrat Hew Skelton Anderson and Edward Strauss, a monocled Jew who had converted to Roman Catholicism (*Memories*, pp. 114–16). But Tommy does not seem to have kept up with the others after leaving Oxford.

in my life', that they were 'very much together' at Oxford, and that
'I retained the same feelings always'.[21]) After a brilliant undergraduate career Harrod became a distinguished economist, and
both he and Tommy befriended the great Cambridge economist
(and Bloomsbury Group member) John Maynard Keynes. In his
biography of Keynes, published in 1951, Harrod recalled Tommy's
'extraordinarily versatile talent' – apart from his accomplishments
as a classicist, and later as a sculptor, he excelled as a poet, an actor,
a pianist, but 'above all a conversationalist' in a 'beautiful, rich,
mellow and appealing voice'. Harrod goes on to eulogise Tommy
in lyrical terms:

> His knowledge was considerable and his mind in incessant
> activity. He had a commanding intellectual power, so that the
> cleverest people were impressed by his judgment, even when
> he was very young… Talk with him was always exhilarating,
> leaving the soul replenished.[22]

In a later book, a memoir of the physicist Professor Lindemann
(later Viscount Cherwell), whom Harrod knew as an academic
colleague at Christ Church, Oxford, Harrod writes again of Tommy,
describing him as 'a very dear friend' and volunteering the reflection
that he (Tommy) 'was inclined to regard homosexuality as a valua-
ble element in society'. Harrod (who knew many of the great men
of the day) adds: 'I would put him above, yes, far above, anyone else
I have known as an entrancing talker.' Though loquacious Tommy
was never boring, because he 'never for a moment forgot the interests and personality of his conversational partner'. When Tommy
stayed with Harrod at Christ Church in the mid-1920s, even the
acidulous and disapproving Lindemann was charmed by him.[23]
But Harrod knew Tommy well enough to be aware of another side
to him – of the 'horrible despair and anguish' which 'seized and
rent him', and made him feel 'personally guilty of all the sufferings
taking place in the world'. The ability to impress and delight was

counterbalanced by a virulent self-hatred – 'it would seem that so much psychical force went into the understanding of others ... that there was no energy left for building up some kind of idea of his own life; when it came to that, he found himself stripped of all vitality, a poor, dejected creature, a broken reed'.[24]

A sonnet Tommy wrote soon after his departure from Oxford, and dedicated to Harrod, suggests that, though not yet out of his teens, he was already leading a promiscuous sex life. Entitled 'On Discussing whether a Man should Dissipate his Power of Delighting in Things, or Concentrate it on One Deserving Object', it may have been designed to assuage Harrod's hurt feelings arising from the fact that Tommy was so free with his favours. Addressed 'to his Creator', it reads:

> When thou dost sit in judgement, Lord, forgive
> If I have loved too many things not well;
> If I do spend all Loving, while I live,
> On all fair things, and have not wit to tell
> What single beauty asks my dearest care;
> If my sweet gold of Love I thinly spread
> I deck a thousand things that I deem fair,
> And make no coronal for one fair head –
> Thine is the fault! For thou hast given to me
> A thousand loves my amorous lips would reach;
> Yet lacks my soul that Love's infinity
> That might afford a royal dower to each...
> This wrong, Unequal Giver, have I done –
> I gave to all, who scarce could spare for one![25]

The religious note was not entirely mocking. Tommy's upbring-ing had been staunchly Anglican;* and his prize poem *Jerusalem*,

---

* His great-grandfather, William Chesshyre, was an eminent clergyman, as was his father's younger brother James Tomlin ('Uncle Jimmy'): both men ended their careers as Canons of Canterbury.

written when he was sixteen, suggests he was a religious school-boy, with an interest in the scriptures. By the time he left Oxford he had probably ceased to hold conventional religious beliefs; but he nevertheless retained what he described – in a letter of 1923 – as 'a religious temperament',[26] and continued to seek (and sometimes to find) a religious meaning to life. (When he later befriended the Bloomsbury Group, he was not afraid to challenge their atheism: Gerald Brenan recalled that he once startled Lytton Strachey by praising 'the Christian spirit'.[27])

Another poem written at this time shows that, notwithstanding the Oxford debacle, Tommy's family still hoped he would read for the bar (as his brother Garrow would later do) and thus enter the profession of his father (now an eminent 'silk'). It is addressed to Leo Myers (1881–1944), a rich Old Etonian dilettante with literary ambitions, then in his late thirties – he would later achieve some renown with five novels (notably a trilogy set in seventeenth-century India), the first of which appeared in 1922. Despite his wealth and socially privileged background, Myers abhorred the British class system and Western materialism, and would later become a Marxist. One way in which he resembled Tommy is that, at the turn of the century, he had prematurely left Trinity College, Cambridge (where his father had been a famous don) without taking a degree, much as Tommy later abandoned his studies at Oxford. How Tommy got to know him is unknown; but it is evident from the poem (reproduced in facsimile in the end-papers to this volume, and transcribed as Appendix I) that Tommy had consulted Myers about his future, and that Myers ('corruptor of my youth') had influenced him with his 'subversive' views. The gist of the verse is that Tommy feels destined to become a poet rather than heed the call of his 'forebears' to 'a moaning at the bar' (an allusion to Tennyson's poem 'Crossing the Bar' – though 'bar' is there used in a nautical rather than a legal sense).[28]

After Oxford, Tommy continued to see much of Sylvia, who

(though far from rich) was welcoming, at her flat in Queens Road, Bayswater, to impecunious Old Harrovians drifting around London – and Tommy was her favourite. As in the past, his vulnerability aroused protective feelings in her. She was enchanted by his good looks, his bohemian outlook, his devil-may-care charm, his cleverness, his inspiring conversation. They would talk and argue for hours, often walking at night. During long evenings in Bayswater they sang duets by Purcell, or composed songs of their own, and Tommy recited verse by his favourite poet, William Blake.[29] The Harrow friend to whom Tommy remained closest was the Anglo-Chilean aspiring actor George Howe, who was joined in London during 1919 by his attractive sister 'Bea'; and Tommy and Sylvia, George and Bea formed something of a 'four-some' who regularly went out for the evening or on out-of-town jaunts together. Sylvia (who would later become a confirmed lesbian) developed romantic feelings for Bea. At the same time she was falling in love with Tommy. This was a dangerous develop-ment; for as Sylvia's biographer writes: 'Tommy admired her very much and valued her as a uniquely entertaining and affectionate friend, but did not return her feelings.'[30] Although they probably made love from time to time (for Tommy aspired to sleep with all his friends at least once), he confided to Bea that he found her physically repulsive.[31]

By the autumn of 1920 Tommy, possibly inspired by his con-templation of the Shelley Memorial, had decided to become a

The Shelley
Memorial

sculptor, and to train with Frank ('Dobbie') Dobson (1886–1963).
How he had come across Dobson we do not know; perhaps they
had met on Tommy's outing to Cornwall in March 1919, as Dobson
then had a studio at Newlyn on the south Cornwall coast, or they
may have been introduced by Leo Myers, a friend and patron of
Dobson. Then in his thirties, a protégé of Augustus John and a
friend of the modernist artist and writer Wyndham Lewis, Dobson
combined serious craftsmanship with a bohemian outlook which
would have appealed to Tommy. He was then mainly known as a
painter, but began to concentrate on sculpture after the war, and
contributed the only sculpture to the Vorticist 'Group X' exhibition
organised by Lewis at London's Mansard Gallery in March 1920.
Despite his flirtation with modernism, he was an essentially
naturalist artist: he is now regarded (along with Jacob Epstein and
Henri Gaudier-Brzeska) as a leading exponent of the transitional

Frank Dobson (right), with Augustus John (left) and Constantin
Brancusi (centre)

phase between the idealistic naturalism of the nineteenth century and the 'new sculpture' of Henry Moore and Barbara Hepworth. He was to become particularly famous for his portrait busts (such as his striking 1922 head of Osbert Sitwell in polished bronze, now in the National Portrait Gallery), whose many admirers included the Bloomsbury critics Roger Fry and Clive Bell.

In October 1920 Dobson wrote to William Rothenstein, the well-known artist who had recently been appointed principal of the Royal College of Art:

> I am threatened with a pupil, a Mr Stephen Tomlin, whose father asked for some authority to whom he could apply for information concerning my ability to train his son as a sculptor. I gave him your name. Of course I don't know what you think of my work, but was prepared to risk that. I hope you don't mind.
>
> I suggested the boy should work with me three mornings a week and spend the remainder of the time drawing at a good school, thinking by that means I should not entirely destroy him.[32]

The reference seems to have been effective, as Tommy started working at Dobson's studio in Manresa Road, Fulham soon afterwards. In a rather scrappy fragment of autobiography (most of his papers, along with many of his pictures, were destroyed by a jealous wife after his death), Dobson affirms that they became great friends. He also recalls a visit they made to Paris, where they enjoyed themselves eating and drinking in the company of Wyndham Lewis and James Joyce, visited galleries featuring works by Bonnard and Picasso, and saw an exhibition of African sculpture at the Trocadéro Museum, which impressed them with its clear and simple lines.[33] Another of Dobson's disciples has written that, during this Paris visit, he (Dobson) was introduced to opium and cocaine, in which he continued to indulge on his return to London, eventually recognising that he had to give them up or suffer ruin as an artist.[34]

It would seem that Tommy also dabbled in these substances, and clung to the habit – which would go some way to explaining the wayward behaviour which marked the rest of his life.

Meanwhile Tommy followed Dobson's advice by attending drawing classes at the Slade School of Fine Art in Bloomsbury: Henry Tonks, the brilliant but sarcastic professor then in charge of that institution, later told one of Tommy's relations that he combined some talent with a curious reluctance to finish any of his work.[35]

At Easter 1921, Tommy, who had just turned twenty, enjoyed a holiday in Dorset with Sylvia, George and Bea, staying at the Weld Arms in East Lulworth and exploring the glorious coastal scenery of the area. After the others had returned to London, Tommy stayed on and hiked five miles west over the Downs, discovering an enchanted village called East Chaldon or Chaldon Herring,[*] tucked into a fold of the hills. To the north was an escarpment marked by Bronze Age burial mounds known as 'the five Marys'; to the south, a few miles of incomparably beautiful downland undulated towards the coastal cliffs. Feeling that both the atmosphere of the place and the contours of the landscape would provide inspiration for his sculpture, he boldly approached the grandest house in the village, the Old Vicarage,[†] and asked the householder, a Mrs Ashburnham, if she knew of a property to rent. Somewhat mesmerised by her visitor, who dressed like a tramp but was clearly a gentleman, she put him in touch with a couple named Wallis, who ran the village pub, The Sailor's Return, and sometimes let out their cottage.[36] Chaldon Herring was to play an important part in the lives of Tommy, Sylvia and many of their friends.

---

[*] So called because William the Conqueror had granted it to a knight named Hareng. From the 1780s to the 1930s the village was part of the Lulworth estate owned by the Weld family.
[†] There had been no vicar since 1917, when the care of St Nicholas's, the village church, had been entrusted to the incumbent of the neighbouring parish of Winfrith.

That Easter, another couple were hiking in Dorset – Rupert Buxton, Tommy's old sparring partner from Harrow, and Michael Llewellyn Davies, one of the 'lost boys' upon whom J. M. Barrie modelled 'Peter Pan'. Soulful and handsome, the two had been inseparable friends since meeting as fellow undergraduates at Christ Church, Oxford in the autumn of 1919. Whether they encountered Tommy during their holiday is not known. But we are told that Tommy was devastated to learn that they had drowned together at Sandford Pool near Oxford just a few weeks later, on 21 May. As the pool was a notoriously treacherous bathing place, it was widely assumed, at the time and afterwards, that they had committed suicide, possibly owing to the hopelessness of continuing their love affair in the social climate of the time. It cannot have failed to strike Tommy, now pursuing the craft of sculpture, that they had suffered the same fate as Shelley, the beautiful statue of whose drowned corpse had so affected him during his own brief Oxford career two years earlier. And Tommy's dismay at the demise of the boy who had inspired Peter Pan assumes a certain irony in view of the fact that he himself, just embarking on his twenties, would show little inclination to keep his feet on the ground.*

* Bea Howe later told a number of people that Tommy had himself been close to Llewellyn Davies, and suffered a breakdown on hearing the news, which was the reason for his leaving Oxford. (Information from Oliver Garnett.) This is of course nonsense: Tommy had abandoned Oxford at least eighteen months before the drowning incident. As for his alleged intimacy with Llewellyn Davies, it is possible that they had known each other as children (they were both brought up in Bayswater); though they are unlikely to have seen much of each other in adolescence, as Llewellyn Davies went to Eton, and only overlapped with Tommy at Oxford (where they were at different colleges) for a few weeks in the spring of 1919. But Tommy would surely have been shocked at the fate of Buxton.

Tommy around the time of his twenty-first birthday, when David Garnett was struck by his 'very broad shoulders, luxuriant fair hair crashed straight back from a fine forehead, crooked nose, deep-set blue eyes ... [and] delightful intimate smile'

II

CHALDON HERRING

1921–1923

In September 1921, after a year's training in sculpture with Frank Dobson in London, Tommy decided to move to Chaldon Herring, the magical hidden corner of Dorset he had discovered the previous Easter, which was to be his principal abode for the next sixteen months. One can but speculate as to his motives in withdrawing from London at the age of twenty to seclude himself for more than a year (including two harsh winters) in one of the most isolated villages in southern England. Was it to dedicate himself to his art? Or to recover from some kind of breakdown, or from a disappointment in love? Or to indulge in the forbidden pleasures of homosexuality or narcotics? For £1 a week he rented the two-bedroomed, whitewashed, heavily thatched cottage (later known as Apple Tree Cottage) of the publican Mr Wallis, where he had already stayed on several short visits during the preceding months. Interviewed sixty years later, the Wallises' daughter recalled that he won the hearts of the village with his charm: 'he could lure the birds off the elm on the village green'.[37] Indeed, he became something of a local legend; when he returned there in May 1926 with the artist Dora Carrington, she wrote to Tommy's future wife Julia Strachey: 'It was rather like travelling with some dethroned King of Bavaria, returning to his long lost country. From every cottage old dames and worthies, children and half-witted hobbled out to kiss the hem of Tommy's corduroy trousers.'[38]

Soon after settling at Chaldon, on a return visit to London to collect his possessions, Tommy told Sylvia Townsend Warner: 'There is a most remarkable man living just beyond the village. He is a sort of hermit, and he has a very fine head. He reads Dostoevsky ... [and] I believe he writes.'[39] This was Theodore Francis Powys (1874–1953), whom Tommy called 'Theo', one of ten gifted children of a wealthy Anglican clergyman who had married a descendant of the poet William Cowper. Along with his elder brother John Cowper Powys and their younger brother Llewellyn, Theo was to achieve fame as a novelist – but all three brothers only gained recognition relatively late in life. Theo had been a farmer in Suffolk; but his farm failed and he returned to live in Dorset where he had been brought up, eventually settling in Chaldon, which he liked for its remoteness, buying a small redbrick villa he named 'Beth Car' (Hebrew for 'the house of the pasture'). In his thirtieth year he married a village girl of eighteen named Violet Dodds: they and their two sons subsisted on a small allowance from Theo's father. Like his siblings, Theo suffered from depression, and he was certainly reclusive: he rarely strayed far from home, only once

Tommy at Chaldon

went abroad (to see the French birthplace of Rabelais), and made just one visit to London (described below). Though his formal education had been patchy, he was formidably well-read, knew the Bible backwards (he wrote in a similar style to the Authorised Version), and was strongly influenced by the philosophy of Nietzsche with its bleak outlook on life. Every day, he wrote, and by the time he met Tommy in 1921, aged forty-seven, he had amassed a considerable corpus of novels and short stories, which combined vivid depictions of rural life with a grim view of human nature; but nothing of his had so far been published apart from *An Interpretation of Genesis*, an eccentric biblical commentary printed privately in 1907, and *The Soliloquy of a Hermit*, a book of philosophical reflections which appeared in 1916. In his *Soliloquy* he argued that, to achieve contentment, one had to lead a life of the greatest simplicity, rejecting not just acquisitiveness but all the excitements of the world. As he put it:

> The simple life – so called – is not the simple life at all; it is the deeper life. The simple life is the life of motor cars, of divorces, of monkey dances, of hunting … of shooting … and playing games… All these things are the natural, the simple life of a man. Anyone can get pleasure in these ways … The best joy is not got quite so easily. I want to cultivate the kind of mind that can turn stones into bread, a dull life into the life of a king. For what we call dullness is really the best soil we can dig in, because the gold that it yields is very precious and very lasting. I would like to know that I am getting rich, not by stealing from the poor, but by getting something more out of myself …[40]

It is not difficult to understand the attraction Theo would have had for Tommy. Here was a man who, like himself, had spurned both a conventional career and the gentry class from which he sprang; whose anti-materialist philosophy struck a chord with him; with whose melancholic tendencies he could sympathise; and

who offered him the affection and understanding he sought in vain
from his own father. Tommy soon became a daily visitor to Beth
Car. After seeing Theo in the summer of 1922, his elder brother
John wrote to their younger brother Llewellyn that he had 'never
left Theodore … in better spirits or better health, largely due to
Mr Tom [*sic*] Tomlin the Sculptor, a bewitching, gipsy-like young
William Blake, with a most caressing respect for Theodore … who
makes the old rogue laugh and chuckle till he's red in the face'.[41]
Tommy had gone to Chaldon at least partly to work on his sculpture, and one of his first sitters was Theo, whose portrait head
(though we know of it only from a photograph) seems to capture
the older man's handsome, brooding features. Tommy persuaded
Theo to show him samples of his extensive unpublished work. He
found this fascinating, though was puzzled that Theo's fiction
showed a disapproving attitude towards sex: in real life (as he wrote
to Sylvia) Theo was 'not in the least Puritanical, in fact just the

Tommy with his bust of T. F. Powys

reverse. He has a distinct streak of Rabelaisian humour and loves to surround himself with all the prettiest girls in the village.'[42]

Tommy set out to help Theo achieve the literary recognition he felt he deserved. He urged him to tidy up his work and render it fit for publication; and meanwhile he put him in contact with Sylvia – this was an inspired move, as Sylvia and Theo, despite their different interests and backgrounds, shared a sense of irony which made them natural soul-mates. At Tommy's suggestion, Sylvia sent Theo a play she had written; Theo responded by sending Sylvia the manuscript of his novel *Mr Tasker's Gods*. Though finding this work, in which most of the characters meet the goriest of ends, somewhat terrifying, Sylvia was 'enthralled' by it and recognised it as 'a work of genius', and soon she and Theo were corresponding enthusiastically. In March 1922 Sylvia visited Tommy at Chaldon and met Theo. This was a success: Sylvia appreciated the whimsical manner Theo adopted with strangers, while Theo, who had never met a bluestocking of Sylvia's type before, found her clever and attractive.[43] Encouraged by the meeting, Theo completed a new novella on which he had been working, *Hester Dominy*, about a schoolmistress who moves from a coastal town to a village resembling Chaldon.* When Tommy next went to London he took the manuscript with him, hoping to interest a publisher in it.

It was during this London visit, in the summer of 1922, that Tommy met a man destined to become his greatest friend – the Bloomsbury bookseller and novelist David Garnett (1892–1981). 'Bunny' (as he was known to friends, owing to a rabbit-fur cap he had worn in childhood) was then twenty-nine, eight years older

* The plot is typical of the author. The heroine is pursued by two suitors, a clergyman and a farmer, but continues to love a tailor she has left behind in the town. She is unaware that the tailor also loves her, and is so stricken by her departure that he has abandoned town life and become a shepherd, close to the village where she now lives. She eventually returns to the town to find him, only to discover that he has just died. Misery is the ultimate lot of all. The story unfolds through a succession of vivid word pictures, and many of the characters speak in dialect.

than Tommy. He was handsome, with wavy hair, an athletic phy-sique and a fine profile, and possessed an animal magnetism which people of both sexes found seductive. Only child of the publisher and critic Edward Garnett and his wife Constance, a celebrated translator of Russian novels, he had had an unusual childhood, during which he experienced little formal schooling but got to know a variety of fascinating people, including D. H. Lawrence and Rupert Brooke. All his life he was intensely romantic; though his dominant instincts were heterosexual, he regarded sex as aris-ing naturally from loving friendship with either men or women. During the First World War he had been a conscientious objector, working as a farm labourer in Sussex with his beloved friend, the Bloomsbury artist Duncan Grant. They lived at Charleston, a farmhouse near Lewes, in a 'love-triangle' with another artist, Vanessa Bell, sister of the future novelist Virginia Woolf; Vanessa was in love with Duncan, and Duncan with Bunny; the bisexual (but men-preferring) Duncan slept with the bisexual (but women-preferring) Bunny and also with Vanessa, the latter liaison resulting in a baby, Angelica, who was accepted by Vanessa's husband, the art critic Clive Bell, as his own, and whom Bunny joked he would one day marry. This Bunny would in fact (to the horror of the girl's biological parents) do many years later; but meanwhile, in 1921, he married Rachel ('Ray') Marshall, an artist and book-illustrator with many connections in the Bloomsbury world: though he always professed to be devoted to her, he conducted numerous affairs, mostly with women but sometimes with men, thoroughout their marriage. After the war, Bunny ran a bookshop in Tavistock Street, Bloomsbury with his longstanding (and very homosexual) friend Francis ('Frankie') Birrell. He had published a novel, *Dope Darling*, which was considered so scandalous that it appeared under a female pseudonym, and was awaiting the publication of a second novel, *Lady into Fox*, which, though quite short, would make him famous overnight and moderately rich.

One afternoon that summer of 1922 an imperious middle-aged lady came into the bookshop, followed by a pale but striking young man with 'very broad shoulders, luxuriant fair hair crashed straight back from a fine forehead, a crooked nose and deep-set blue eyes. A delightful intimate smile played about his mouth.' Bunny came forward, and the lady announced: 'We want to look at some books on *modern art*. My son was told this was a good place to find such things.' Bunny produced some French periodicals on the subject. Tommy (for it was he) exclaimed delightedly that this was just the sort of thing he was looking for, and begged his mother to proceed on her own to the tea party to which he was accompanying her, where he would join her in half an hour. As Tommy escorted her out of the shop, put her in a taxi and waved her farewell, Bunny was struck by his affectionate manner towards her: 'He had treated her as tenderly as a lover.' (This suggests that Tommy suffered from an Oedipus complex.) This encounter (which opens the third volume of his memoirs) was clearly one of the great moments of Bunny's life; and though he wrote (in the early 1960s) at a time when homosexuality remained dangerously illegal, he makes little secret of how seductive he found his latest customer.

> The young man's charm was obvious: it was the thing one noticed as soon as he spoke or laughed, and he was always laughing. When I got to know him well I realised that there was no one ... whose laughter expressed a greater range of emotions. Tenderness, indulgence, confession, apology, accusation, forgiveness, criticism: all such states of mind were expressed in laughter: besides which he would laugh long and loud and merrily, or with tragic bitterness.
>
> At this meeting I was first aware of his charm, then of a penetrating mature intelligence. We were alone in the shop ... we at once forgot that he had come to buy ... and, by closing time, the talk had ranged from Malliol, Gaudier and Brancusi

[the contemporary sculptors Tommy regarded as role-models]
to Blake, Dostoevsky and the French unanimists.[44]

Bunny writes that he then went home to his wife, while Tommy
went to join his mother an hour and a half late. But writing to
Sylvia Townsend Warner in 1927, he recalled that he and Tommy
met again for dinner that evening, 'at Gustave's'. As he says, they
had become 'interested in each other'.[45]

Tommy then returned to Chaldon. Having learnt that Bunny
had strong connections in the publishing world (and was himself
the partner of a small firm specialising in reprints of the classics,
The Nonesuch Press), he arranged for Sylvia to call at the bookshop
with the manuscript of *Hester Dominy*. The encounter between
Sylvia and Bunny was later recalled with amusement by them
both. Sylvia remembered 'an extremely young-looking man whose
hair was long and thick and untidy and whose suit was so blue that
I felt he might blow his horn at any moment. When I entered he
retreated behind a desk, like some innocent wild animal.'[46] Bunny
remembered 'an alarming lady with a clear and minatory voice,
dark, dripping with tassels … with jingling earrings, swinging fox-
tails, black silk acorn hanging to umbrella, black tasselled gloves,
dog-chains, key-rings … speaking to me in sentences like scissors.'[47]
They became instant friends. Bunny was impressed by *Hester
Dominy*. As he later wrote in a review: 'The story is an absolutely
satisfactory work of art … and the author seems to me to be one of
the very small number who take writing seriously and have some
idea about it.'[48] He wrote to Theo to express his admiration of the
piece, and his desire to help. This elicited a reply from Tommy:
'Dear Garnett, Theodore Powys came to see me very pleased and
excited by your letter about "Hester Dominy". I am so glad you
like it.' He invited Bunny to spend a weekend at Chaldon to meet
the author and see 'this the most excellent village in England'.[49]
Bunny accepted, and visited Tommy in September.

In his memoirs, Bunny describes the weekend (probably the
first of several) – but, writing forty years after the event, his memory
is at fault. He says it took place in the depths of winter, whereas it
was the late summer; he implies that Tommy had just moved to the
village, whereas he had been living there for almost a year. Other
details are probably accurate, such as Tommy meeting him at the
station at Wool, their trekking over the downs to Chaldon, and
the sparse furnishings of Tommy's cottage. He notes that Tommy
was loved and cherished by the two most notable residents of the
village, the rather comical Mrs Ashburnham at the Old Vicarage
and the intensely serious Theo Powys at Beth Car, even though the
latter could not abide the former. What fascinated him about Theo
was the contrast between his evidently shrewd, censorious mind
and the humble, polite manner he used to protect himself from the
world.[50] What Bunny does not say in his memoirs – but confided
to Sylvia in 1927 – is that, during the weekend, his intimacy with
Tommy blossomed: 'I was too much charmed and delighted with
Tommy to consider Chaldon and its inhabitants as more than a
setting fit for him.'[51] Tommy's next letter to Bunny, dated 4 October,
ends: 'There are lots of soul stirring things I want to say to you… I
am glad you liked being here. If you enjoyed it half as much as
I enjoyed – you know the formula … but I mean it. I like you. Love
Tommy'[52] (This may not sound effusive: but it should be borne
in mind that men, when they wrote to each other lovingly, had to
be circumspect in letters.) Certainly if the weekend did not mark
the start of a love affair between Bunny and Tommy it paved the
way for that development: for when, a few years later, his wife
reproached him for his marital infidelity, Bunny reminded her that
she had not been 'jealous about Tommy'.[53] Though we have no
details, it seems certain that they had further meetings that autumn,
either in London or Chaldon: when, in the new year of 1923,
Tommy took a studio in London, the first project he completed
was a portrait head of Bunny carved in Ham Hill stone.

The fact that Tommy's dearest wish was to see Theo's work published was no doubt a spur to Bunny to advance this project; for though preoccupied with the publication of his own *Lady into Fox*, which appeared that October to some sensation, and with his wife's pregnancy, he went out of his way to help. He recommended *Hester Dominy* to the publisher of *Lady into Fox*, Charles Prentice of Chatto & Windus, who liked the piece but thought it too short to stand as a book. However, after Theo had supplied two further stories, *The Left Leg* and *Abraham Men*, Prentice agreed to publish the three together. They appeared in May 1923 as *The Left Leg*: Theo dedicated them individually to Bunny, Sylvia and Tommy. The book (as with all Theo's subsequent books) was also taken by an American publisher, Knopf. And it was thanks to Bunny that the literary editor H. N. Brailsford, a friend of his parents, became interested in Theo's work and over the next four years published no fewer than twenty of Theo's stories in his periodical *New Leader*. Bunny also persuaded his father, the principal 'reader' at Jonathan Cape, to read Theo's novel *Mr Tasker's Gods*, which had so terrified

David 'Bunny' Garnett

Sylvia: Garnett Senior liked it but thought it too scary for their readers and urged Theo to rewrite and modify it. (Theo did so, and the book was issued by Chatto and Knopf in 1925.)[54] Writing to Roy Harrod in the autumn of 1923, Tommy declared himself 'very proud and pleased' to have achieved so much for his friend.[55]

Apart from his relationship with Theo we know little about Tommy's life at Chaldon. Presumably he dedicated himself to his sculpture, though no work from this period appears to survive. He also did some writing: together with Theo, he contrived a one-act play, *The Sin Eater* (later performed privately, with sets designed by Tommy).* Apart from Sylvia and Bunny, other friends came to stay with him in his cottage – his schoolmate Gerald Gardiner, now a leading light of the Oxford University Dramatic Society; Roy Harrod, completing his studies at New College with a 'double first' and on the threshold of a brilliant academic career; George and Bea Howe. We know of no local friends he made apart from Theo and Mrs Ashburnham, though there must have been some. He drank regularly at the village pub, The Sailor's Return; and he no doubt found pleasure with local maidens and swains. He certainly spent countless hours rambling on the downs. From time to time he returned to London – which involved an hour's brisk hike to Wool, followed by a three-hour train journey – though there is no indication of how regularly these visits took place, or (except for the encounter with Bunny) what he did when he got there.

However, Bunny was just one of several exciting new friends who now lured him back to the capital; and although he would often return to the village (starting the following Whitsun), in January 1923 he gave up his cottage to resume London life. 'I seriously do

---

* Sin-eating was 'the consumption of a collection of cold scraps, peelings and bits of hair to dispose mystically of a dead man's sins'. Soon afterwards, Sylvia composed a play of her own on the subect: it is unclear whether this was based on the Powys-Tomlin script, or was an entirely new work, and whether the 'staged' version was Tommy's or Sylvia's. (Harman, *Sylvia Townsend Warner*, pp. 54–5.)

not suppose I shall ever again be so continuously happy, or tap such a deep well of contentment, as in my Chaldon sojourn', he wrote to Theo soon after his departure, 'and in a great part the happiness came from you.' Sadly, his bust of Theo 'fell irrevocably to pieces' in the course of the move to the metropolis.[56] Though it had lasted little more than a year, Tommy's residence at Chaldon had stupendous consequences for the village. The publication of *The Left Leg* put the formerly unknown Theo on the literary map, and was followed by three novels, *Black Bryony* (1923), *Mr Tasker's Gods* (1925) and *Mr Weston's Good Wine* (1927), which consolidated his reputation. In 1925, David Garnett published a novel, *The Sailor's Return*, set in a village modelled on Chaldon and mostly written while staying at the Chaldon pub of that name. (Also in 1925, on Tommy's recommendation, another sculptor who had been apprenticed to Frank Dobson, the Canadian Elizabeth Muntz, came to work in Chaldon, renting and finally buying the cottage formerly occupied by Tommy.) And in 1930, Sylvia, by then a celebrated novelist, would settle there with her new partner, the young poetess Valentine Ackland, Chaldon subsequently providing the setting for much of her poetry and fiction. (Also in 1930, Tommy was responsible for the writer Gerald Brenan visiting Chaldon, where he met his future wife, the American poet Gamel Woolsey, who had been having an affair with Theo's locally living brother Llewellyn.) Previously unknown to the public, Chaldon became (and remains to this day) a magnet for literary tourists. As Tommy later wrote to Theo: 'It has been a joy to hear of Chaldon & its inhabitants … It now seems to be the best known village in England. Theo dear, we ought to have kept it a secret. But it would be hard to find a bushel sufficiently large and opaque enough to hide a light like yours.'[57]

There was a curious postscript to Tommy's 'Chaldon sojourn'. In December 1923 the Powyses' eldest son Dicky, having left Sherborne school, was due to sail for Kenya to work on the farm of Theo's brother William (where he would die a few years later).

Tommy persuaded Theo and Violet to visit London, where neither of them had ever been, to see him off at Tilbury docks. He did so with some difficulty, as the very idea of London filled them with 'black terrors': in particular they were appalled by the prospect of the London traffic, Violet declaring that the sight of a double-decker bus in Dorchester had made her feel sick. However, Tommy was determined that they should go, and to ensure they did so spent most of November with them in Chaldon, and escorted them to the capital, where they stayed in Chiswick with Theo's younger brother A. R. Powys, architect, writer and founder of the Society for the Preservation of Ancient Buildings. The visit was something of a nightmare for the poor Powyses. Being used to the simplest diet, they found the rich food of Soho restaurants indigestible; and having led an isolated existence, they were bewildered by the parties in their honour arranged by Tommy, Sylvia and Bunny. They nevertheless behaved graciously on these occasions, the highlights of which were a lunch to introduce Theo to Arnold Bennett and Lytton Strachey, a dinner given by Sylvia at her flat on her thirtieth birthday, and a huge party thrown by Tommy at his studio, at which Theo, to show that 'the pen is mightier than the sword', was invited to cut a cake representing a 'left leg' with a giant nib.[58]

Tommy never forgot Theo. In 1933 he learnt that the Powyses, having been deprived of their small private income by Theo's father's death, had fallen into penury. Though Tommy himself was going rapidly downhill at this time, and had not long to live, he managed – through the influence of Augustus John and Bunny – to get Theo awarded a pension from the Civil List, which sustained the novelist for the remaining two decades of his life.[59]

Tommy in his Fernshaw Road studio with one of his sculptures: the fig-leaf
painted on the wall to cover up Bunny's list of his lovers is visible top right

III

HENRIETTA

1923–1925

On his return to London from Chaldon in the New Year of 1923, Tommy took the lease of a spacious studio in Fernshaw Road, Fulham,[*] not far from Manresa Road where he had trained with Frank Dobson (with whom he continued to associate both socially and professionally[†]). He got down to work on a 'more than life-sized bust' of his new great friend Bunny Garnett – unusually, this was not modelled in clay, his usual medium, but carved in Ham Hill stone. Bunny's pocket diary shows that they met almost daily during the first ten weeks of the year – most of these meetings were no doubt portrait sittings, but they seem to have been intensely wrapped up in each other at the time, and it is accepted by the Garnett family that they had a physical affair, though this soon transmuted into a lasting romantic friendship.

Close though it was, there was nothing exclusive about the relationship. Bunny attended to his wife Ray, who gave birth to

---

[*] An advertisement for the studio, placed by Tommy in the weekly *Nation and Athenaeum* when he later tried to sublet it, reads: 'Large Studio, Furnished; bedroom (h. & c. laid on); use of bathroom; electric and gas range, &c.' He wanted three and a half guineas a week for the property – a considerable sum at the time. (Tommy to David Garnett, 1 November 1923 [Northwestern University].)

[†] The Canadian sculptor Elizabeth Muntz, at this time training with Dobson in his studio, noted several visits from Tommy in her diary in the early months of 1923. She found him 'very gay', 'delightful', 'a nice boy'. His apprearances there seem to have been more social than professional: on one occasion he played *The Beggar's Opera* on the studio piano, while everyone sang along. (Elizabeth Muntz diary in Dorchester County Museum, with thanks to Carol Graham.)

Tommy's portrait head of
David 'Bunny' Garnett

their first son, Richard, on 8 January, and was also having a serious flirtation with Mina Kirstein, a young American college professor he had met during the autumn. As for Tommy, during their daily sittings he talked freely about his love life, and Bunny was amazed: as he writes in his memoirs, his own amorous progress 'had sometimes been rather involved, but it was nothing to Tommy's. There can never have been a young man so run after and so unfailingly charming to all his pursuers.' Bunny illustrates the point with a striking anecdote. One day he turned up for a sitting to find Tommy out; he let himself in (he seems to have had his own key), and amused himself by scribbling on the wall a list of 'those in whose company Tommy might have had the best of reasons for forgetting his appointment with me'. A few days later, 'a long-sighted young woman' visiting the studio noticed the list, and demanded to know 'how her name came to be written there and what the other persons had in common with herself and each other'. Tommy, while making no attempt to deny the list's veracity to Bunny, treated it as a joke and entered into the spirit by painting a large fig-leaf over it.[60]

Presumably, Bunny's 'list' included men as well as women. Writing his memoirs in the early sixties when homosexuality remained illegal, he makes no direct reference to this; but there is (in the view of his biographer) an implied reference, when Bunny remarks that Tommy reminded him of the angel in a poem by Blake:

> I asked a thief to steal me a peach,
> He turned up his eyes,
> I asked a little lady to lay her down,
> Holy and meek she cries.

As soon as I went
An Angel came:
He wink'd at the thief,
And smil'd at the dame;

And without one word said
Had a peach from the tree,
And still as a maid,
Enjoyed the lady.

The downy peach evokes a youth's buttocks; and Bunny seems to be hinting that, through the exercise of charm, Tommy had all the boys he wanted as well as girls.[61] The writer and hispanicist Gerald Brenan, who met Tommy the following year, described him as an 'ambisexual' who 'went to bed with anyone and everyone, often merely for the sake of company'.[62] (Brenan himself was resolutely heterosexual and resistant to Tommy's charms – though it will be seen that they did once go to bed together, under somewhat unusual circumstances, in 1932.)

Flushed with the royalties of *Lady into Fox*, Bunny decided to throw a great party for his thirtieth birthday on 9 March 1923 (which fell one week after Tommy's twenty-second birthday). For the occasion he borrowed the studio in Fitzroy Street (formerly used by Whistler and Sickert) of his close friend and former lover Duncan Grant – a large space open to the roof rafters 'like a big boat upside down'. This is a key moment in our story, for the guests, apart from Duncan, included Clive and Vanessa Bell; Leonard and Virginia Woolf; Lytton Strachey and his companion, the artist Dora Carrington; and Maynard Keynes and his future wife, the ballerina Lydia Lopokova. This was the core of what was then famous (and to some notorious) as 'the Bloomsbury Group' – and it is probable that Tommy was meeting most of these people (some of whom he would soon get to know intimately) for the first time.

'Bloomsbury' had begun as a set of clever and idealistic under-graduates at Cambridge at the start of the century, including Lytton Strachey, Clive Bell, Leonard Woolf, Saxon Sydney-Turner, Morgan Forster, the brothers Thoby and Adrian Stephen, and John Maynard Keynes. They were in revolt against Victorian values; they had a passion for intellectual argument; they set great store by the pursuit of truth, and honesty in personal relationships; and they were strongly influenced by the philosophy of G. E. Moore, with its notion of promoting 'the good' (which Moore partly equated with the pursuit of love and the aesthetic appreciation of art). In 1904, around the time these men left Cambridge, the Stephen brothers, along with their sisters Vanessa and Virginia, moved (following the death of their father, the Victorian sage Leslie Stephen) to Gordon Square, Bloomsbury; other members of the set settled nearby and they often met in each other's houses for evenings of discussion. They were joined by some older figures, such as the literary critic Desmond MacCarthy and the art critic Roger Fry, and some younger ones, such as Lytton Strachey's brother James and cousin Duncan Grant (and – just before the outbreak of war in 1914 – Bunny Garnett). The fraternity suffered a setback with the death of Thoby Stephen in 1906, but became more closely bound with the marriages of Clive Bell to Vanessa in 1907, and Leonard Woolf to Virginia in 1912. They first came to public attention over the furore surrounding the Post-Impressionist Exhibitions of 1910 and 1912, which were organised by Roger Fry with the help of Clive and Leonard, and championed in the salons and literary reviews by other members of the 'Group'. During the First World War they stood out by resisting the tide of aggressive patriotism engulfing the country, which won them many enemies but some new friends, including Bertrand Russell and Lady Ottoline Morrell; several of them (including Duncan and Bunny) were conscientious objectors.

The Group (though its membership and philosophy were never

closely defined) flourished in the aftermath of the war. Roger Fry and Clive Bell were the country's leading art critics; Desmond McCarthy was a leading literary editor; Lytton Strachey and Virginia Woolf emerged as celebrated writers (Morgan Forster having already attained celebrity); the Hogarth Press, run by Leonard and Virginia, became an influential publisher; Duncan and Vanessa were among the leading modern artists; and Keynes's *The Economic Consequences of the Peace* established him as one of the world's leading economists. Two of the younger members – Adrian Stephen and James Strachey – became psychoanalysts, and helped disseminate Freud's ideas in England (James, assisted by his wife Alix, would later produce the English edition of Freud's collected writings). But the hostility to them burgeoned too. Apart from attracting opprobrium for their opposition to the war, they were attacked as an exclusive and self-promoting coterie who led comfortable upper-middle-class existences while espousing left-wing values. They also aroused disapproval (even among some who otherwise shared their liberal social and political outlook, such as D. H. Lawrence) for their wholehearted acceptance of homosexuality and bisexuality (though only a few of them – notably Lytton, Morgan, Duncan and, until his forties, Maynard – were seriously 'gay').

This was the gilded constellation with which Tommy came into contact through Bunny. Though their many enemies included Frank Dobson's friend Wyndham Lewis, who bore a grudge against them following a quarrel with Roger Fry in 1913, there was much about them that made them enormously attractive to Tommy, and him equally attractive to them – their love of intellectual discussion; their bohemian lifestyles, and free sexual *mores*; their rejection of conventional values, and of sentimentality in art. He appealed to them with his charm, intellect and good looks, and was destined to be a sought-after guest at their parties and gatherings. He was by nature suited to participate in the 'multiple relationships' with which their world abounded. The fact that they were all

Duncan Grant (left) and
John Maynard Keynes (right)

older than Tommy (by a couple of decades, in most cases) was no
bar to friendship – indeed, as Tommy had difficult relations with
his own parents, he came in a sense to regard them as a collection
of substitute fathers and mothers (though some of them, notably
Virginia Woolf, were unsuited to assume this protective role).

Although Bunny's party of March 1923 marked Tommy's introduction to Bloomsbury *en masse*, two of those attending he already
knew – Duncan Grant and Maynard Keynes (who had themselves
conducted a long love affair before the war). Duncan, an attractive
gay man of thirty-seven, had become amorously involved eighteen
months earlier with Tommy's Harrow friend and paramour Angus
Davidson, then a Cambridge undergraduate (and now a Bloomsbury resident). Through this connection, Duncan met Tommy:
in January 1923, he told Vanessa Bell (with whom he lived in a
close platonic relationship at Charleston) that he was off to see
a pantomime with Angus and Tommy. Duncan was soon added to
the long list of Tommy's lovers: 'You are at the moment no doubt
sitting in the arms of Tommy', Vanessa wrote to him in April
1923.[63] (Duncan in reply admitted to fancying Tommy, but added
perceptively that 'he ought to be careful about his nerves ... he
leads a very rackety life but then he's very sorry'.[64]) Maynard,

A drawing of Tommy by Duncan Grant, probably done early in 1923 and inscribed 'to Angus from Duncan'

then thirty-nine, had been introduced to Tommy by Roy Harrod (who, following his election as a fellow of Christ Church, Oxford in 1922, had obtained leave to spend the autumn of that year under Keynes's academic wing at King's College, Cambridge). Although Keynes certainly found Tommy attractive, and they probably had a sexual fling, their affair is likely to have been brief; for Maynard was already contemplating a married future with Lydia (who entranced Bunny's party by arriving from her performance at Covent Garden and dancing a *pas seul*), and at her behest was in the process of disentangling himself from his last serious male lover, the young Cambridge psychologist Sebastian Sprott. It was probably through Tommy that Maynard met Frank Dobson, whom Maynard commissioned to sculpt a widely admired bust of Lydia during the autumn of 1923.

Apart from the Bloomsbury contingent, there was another person Tommy met at Bunny's party who was to dominate his life over the next couple of years, and thanks to whom he would experience the extremes of ecstasy and agony – the tall and comely American heiress Henrietta Bingham. Bunny wrote of her that 'her beauty and the strength of her personality were such that she usually dominated any group of people among whom she found herself', and this was certainly the case at his party, where she held the attention of all by singing the negro spiritual *Water Boy* in a husky Southern voice.[65] We know quite a lot about the relationship which ensued, for Tommy, normally a poor correspondent, addressed a stream of letters to her, most of which she kept. Indeed, thanks to the biography of Henrietta by her great-niece Emily Bingham, published in 2015, we know far more about her early life and the influences which shaped it than we do about Tommy's.[66]

Henrietta was two months older than Tommy, having been born in Louisville, Kentucky in January 1901. Her father, an attorney, held minor elective judicial office for a few years, being known thereafter as 'Judge Bingham'. Her mother came from a wealthy Southern industrial family. Henrietta had an older and a younger brother, both of whom were unsatisfactory – the elder became an alcoholic while still in his teens, the younger suffered from a paralysing shyness. The family's hopes were centered on Henrietta, a robust, attractive girl with much natural charm. Her upbringing, however, was affected by a series of traumatic events. When she was twelve, she and her mother were travelling in a motor car when her uncle who was driving (and who suffered from poor eyesight) managed to manoeuvre the vehicle onto a railway line and into the path of an oncoming train. Henrietta survived but her mother was mortally injured before her eyes. Her father was devastated by his loss and turned to his daughter for comfort, and there ensued a relationship which may to some extent have been incestuous in character. In 1916, to Henrietta's consternation, her father took as his second wife Mary Lily Flager, a widow who was one of the richest women in America. Henrietta, who did not conceal her dislike of her stepmother, was packed off to boarding school. However, just seven months into the marriage, Mary Lily died in mysterious circumstances: her husband was away at the time, but had left her under the care of doctors he had instructed. Mary Lily had indeed suffered from chronic ill-health as a result of addiction to both alcohol and morphine, but the treatment she received during her last days was strange indeed. Though the police did not pursue a criminal investigation, it was widely rumoured that the Judge had 'arranged' her demise – especially when it emerged that, although he had signed a pre-nuptial declaration promising to make no claims on her estate, she had, shortly before her death, made a codicil to her will leaving him five million dollars. The Judge used his new wealth to buy a mass-circulation newspaper, the *Courier-Journal*, the skilful management of which enabled him not only to increase his fortune but also to acquire political influence, which he exercised in favour of the Democratic Party. He also purchased a grand estate on the Ohio River near Louisville, including an imposing neo-Georgian mansion built in 1911, which he renamed 'Melcombe Bingham' (after a famous property in Dorset which he claimed had belonged to his relations).

Although she had trouble reading and writing (she was probably dyslexic), Henrietta was accepted in 1920, aged nineteen, by a prestigious women's university, Smith College in Massachusetts. Once there, however, she experienced difficulties with her studies, and felt lonely and depressed. Seeking help and protection, she drew close to the youngest of her teachers, Mina Kirstein, the clever and beautiful daughter, then twenty-four, of a rich Jewish storeowner. Mina was beguiled by Henrietta and willingly assumed this protective role, and before long the two were locked in a passionate (though necessarily clandestine) lesbian affair. The instigator of this seems to have been Henrietta, who had already had a string of lesbian relationships at her boarding school, as well as with a sophisticated older woman in Louisville: Mina, despite being a woman of 'advanced' social and political views, seems to have been new to such experiences, which, though she was in love with Henrietta, filled her with guilt and unease. Meanwhile Mina met and impressed Judge Bingham, and persuaded him that Henrietta would benefit from a year in England, guided by herself; having obtained a sabbatical for this purpose, she joined Henrietta in London in the summer of 1922. During the Atlantic crossing she met the New York psychiatrist A. A. Brill, who recommended a course of psychoanalysis with Sigmund Freud's leading English acolyte, Dr Ernest Jones. By the end of the year, the two women were living at a flat in Mayfair and having regular (and fabulously expensive) sessions in Harley Street with Jones, who (holding the orthodox Freudian view that homosexuality was an essentially psychopathic condition) was fascinated by their 'case' and achieved a somewhat sinister ascendency over them. It was also around this time that Mina met Bunny (like Tommy, by going into Birrell and Garnett's bookshop), and they embarked on their close friendship (which seems to have been largely platonic); having met Henrietta on visits to Mina, Bunny asked them both to his party on 9 March.

Tommy's sexual appetite may have become jaded by his myriad conquests, but he had never met anyone quite like Henrietta and became instantly infatuated with her. The day after the party he wrote to her begging to see her again; they met in a foursome with Bunny and Mina, but not long afterwards she came alone to his studio, and for the next three months they conducted a passionate affair, probably Henrietta's first serious affair with a man (though it was not an exclusive relationship – Henrietta continued cohabiting with Mina, while Tommy was intermittently sleeping with Duncan). 'I love you', Tommy wrote to her. 'You are the best companion I have ever had and the most desirable lover. I have never known anyone with beauty like yours – that drives me nearly mad and yet fills me with deep content. I want you so.'[67] In another letter he wrote that if she came 'to live with me now and we both lived to be 80 I should still not have sufficient time really to explore you'.[68] They spent their evenings together either at the theatre (where they had access to the best seats thanks to Henrietta's *Courier-Journal* press pass), or at clubs such as the Blue Lantern which performed the jazz and black musicals which were just becoming fashionable in London, but which Henrietta had long loved. They also motored together round the country: letters mention visits to Brighton, Romney Marsh and the Malvern Hills, and Tommy took her to Chaldon where the entire village turned out to see her. Artistically, Tommy devoted himself that spring

Tommy's bust of Henrietta

to working on a bust of her: gazing downwards, and tilted to one side, the head captures an elusive, coquettish, quizzical quality.

One thing which drew them together was that they had both suffered, in the course of their young lives, from psychological problems. (We know far more about Henrietta's than Tommy's.) They confided in each other about the traumas they had endured, and Tommy, who fancied himself something of an amateur psychologist, was fascinated to hear about Henrietta's psychoanalysis. Henrietta suggested that Tommy himself undergo a course of analysis with Dr Jones, but Tommy said he would never be able to afford the fees, and would not hear of Henrietta paying. Meanwhile Jones, when informed by his patient about her heterosexual romance, declared that he considered it a thoroughly healthy development and encouraged her to continue with it. In a number of letters to her (mostly written after her return to America), Tommy attempted to analyse his own feelings for her. In his amorous career so far (he was still just twenty-two) he had been 'an egotist' and a seducer; but now he was 'badly in love',[69] the familiar situation was reversed, and he found himself dependent on her for his happiness. 'If only I could cultivate that healthy contempt for you that becomes the amorous male! But you have robbed me of it & filled me with an abject admiration of you that makes me dumb & foolish.'[70] 'I believe "making love" depends on a sense of superiority over the object of your desire, but "being in love" on a sense of inferiority to it. So that once you are "in love" you cannot "make love", & so cannot make the other party love you. Which is … a dilemma in which I find myself for the first time.' 'You got me on my knees at the start & I suppose that is where I shall remain … a position I am not at all accustomed to.'[71] Under the circumstances, his passion for her was mixed with anxiety; for although he worshipped and longed for her, he knew she was bound to tire of him sooner or later (indeed, his abject and possessive attitude towards her was likely to hasten this development).

To Tommy's chagrin, the relationship entered a more subdued phase when, during June, Henrietta was joined in London by her father and brothers. For three months he had had her largely to himself; he would now see less of her. Mina's mother and brothers came over at the same time, and the two women moved out of their Mayfair flat into Grove House, a regency villa in Chelsea a short distance from Tommy's studio in Fulham, with ample space to accommodate the two families. One fine evening around midsummer Henrietta and Mina threw a party there, spilling out of french windows from the drawing room to the garden, to which they invited most of the people they had met at Bunny's party three months earlier: the moment later recalled by all was Henrietta's introduction of the black American blues singer Edith Wilson to Judge Bingham – back in Kentucky, they would never have been able to meet socially, but they got on well and remained talking for some time.[72] Henrietta subsequently presented her father with a bronze cast of Tommy's bust of her, and the Judge responded by commissioning Tommy to design gateposts for Melcombe Bingham surmounted by a pair of sculpted stone eagles. Despite this amiable gesture, Tommy was depressed that he was now rarely able to be alone with her (living nearby though she was), and that the Judge was insisting that she return with him to America at the end of August. The occasions when Tommy joined Henrietta *en famille* tended to be sticky: Bunny wrote to Mina of an evening when he, Tommy and the Binghams drove to dine at a hotel near Guildford; despite Tommy's desperate attempts to make conversation ('Do counties in America vary much in size?'), the judge remained almost silent during the journey, while Henrietta 'looked murderous'.[73]

Finally the dreaded day of Henrietta's departure arrived – 25 August. Tommy saw her off at Southampton; just before the ship sailed, she threw him a *billet-doux* over the railings. 'O darling it was horrible', he wrote to her. 'I thought the way I loved you was so quiet & profound that I shouldn't really be upset by your going away.'[74] They had been together for almost six months. She had promised to return to England to be with him as soon as she could, possibly after Christmas.

Deprived of Henrietta, Tommy was miserable. He felt (as he later told Bunny) as if all his teeth had fallen out,[75] and now recognised only two states of existence – of being with her, and not with her. As often happened at moments of depression or stress, he disappeared from view. Bunny, staying at a house party which included Maynard Keynes, had no idea where he was, but guessed that he might have retreated to Chaldon; Keynes insisted they drive all the way to Chaldon to see him, but he was not there.[76] (This suggests that Keynes was then infatuated with Tommy.) In fact Tommy had gone to stay with his parents, who were renting a property near Taunton for the late summer. Whereas Tommy had recently been hobnobbing with a prospective father-in-law who used the honorary title of 'judge', his own father was now the genuine article, having been appointed a judge of the Chancery Division of the High Court, with a knighthood. As usual, Thomas Tomlin was in despair about his son; and he warned him that, now he was giving up his large earnings at the Bar for a judge's fixed salary, he would be less able to support his children financially. (At this time he gave Tommy a weekly allowance of £3, worth about £165 in the values of a century later, and advanced additional sums to pay for such things as the lease of his studio and the casting of his sculptures.) Tommy continued to receive moral support from his mother, who a few weeks earlier had written to Henrietta: 'You can't think how grateful I am to you and your father for having given Tommy his first orders [the gatepost eagles]. It has meant so much to him and been such a great encouragement ... There is nothing in the world I want so much as for Tommy to make a success of his art & sometimes I fear he does not realise how fast the years slip by – artists only work when they are in the mood for it, unless faced with starvation. His hard-working father finds this very irritating! Thank you for your kindness and friendship for the boy, he has had such a happy time with you.'[77]

On leaving his parents, Tommy spent a week as Duncan's guest at Charleston. 'A lovely place', he wrote to Henrietta. 'I did several walks with Duncan & played bull-fights with the children [Julian and Quentin Bell, aged fourteen and twelve, and their sister Angelica, just five] & talked to Vanessa & Clive & laughed at Clive's jokes & painted some horrible pictures... Virginia & Leonard [living nearby at Rodmell] came over one day & Virginia read a very amusing one-act play she has written.'[78] Back in London, he made regular visits to London Zoo, studying and drawing the eagles for his Bingham commission. He admitted to Henrietta that his head had been turned by 'the most bewitching young Frenchman, a bookseller and painter'; but the receipt of a letter from her had 'let loose the dogs of longing at my vitals once again'.[79] One thing which comforted him was the company of his surviving brother Garrow. After graduating from Cambridge in 1921 with a degree in engineering, Garrow had gone to work in the Venezuelan oilfields; but by September 1923 he was back in England, where he reluctantly succumbed to family pressure and began reading for the Bar. The two brothers (Garrow was the elder by three years) shared a strong sex-drive, a love of conversation and a tendency to melancholy, but were otherwise very different. Tommy was short, attractive, and perfectly put together. He was blessed with charm, and quickly won over most of those he met. Garrow was tall and rugged, with (as Bunny put it) 'a touch of the anthropoid-ape or cave man about him',[80] his looks marred by an oversized jaw. He possessed an aggressive manner which tended

Tommy (right) with his brother Garrow and their sister Helen

to alienate people. Whereas Tommy was a born seducer who had little difficulty in getting most of what he wanted, Garrow longed for success with women but usually put them off: for years he pressed his unwelcome attentions on Bunny's sister-in-law, Frances Marshall, with whom he had become infatuated at Cambridge. (Though clearly preferring women, Garrow nevertheless seems, like Tommy, to have been bisexual: the artist Robert Medley claimed in his memoirs that Garrow, seven years his senior, 'after dinner in Lamb's Conduit Street [Holborn], was the first person ever to seduce me'.[81]) Despite these differences the two brothers

Tommy at Chaldon with his bust of Garrow, November 1923

were devoted to each other; and as frustrated love seems to have been Garrow's natural condition, he was able to sympathise with Tommy in his heartache over Henrietta.

By November Tommy was back in Chaldon, where (as he wrote to Roy Harrod) he was trying to 'recapture peace' after a 'pretty distressing' time.[82] He was joined there for a time by Garrow, of whom he sculpted a portrait head. Early December saw the visit to London, overseen by Tommy, of Theo and Violet Powys, described in the previous chapter. Throughout the last weeks of 1923, Tommy addressed a stream of passionate letters to Henrietta, assuring her how much he adored and missed her; but Henrietta's replies were brief and rare, and he was in an agony of uncertainty about her feelings for him. She did send him occasional presents (a hamper of food from her father's farm in Georgia, silk pyjamas for Chrismas), and Tommy got indirect news of her through Mina's regular letters to Bunny. Through this channel, he learned that December that Henrietta was wondering whether he would 'consider marrying' her. He wrote to her in response: 'Come back, my darling, in January as you said you would. And then, if you really think you know all about me and have no illusions, O let's get married. But I only want to see you again – that's the great thing, to see you and kiss you.' And he told her about a 'recurring dream' he had had about her:

> It begins in an ordinary sexual way. I am always conscious of being in a strange place, America perhaps, or some house you have taken me to. You at first are always lovable and nude. Later I dress you, usually in the same rather surprising and beautiful dress (once it was a very elaborate and be-flounced riding habit). Then you begin to reproach me with some trivial neglect or other, not angrily but persistently … and I am conscious of contentment that your rebukes cannot disturb my happiness, when I have you before me to delight and admire.[83]

Henrietta did not come to London that January, when she had her own troubles to contend with. In the fall of 1923 Mina had resumed her professorship at Smith College, where Henrietta (who had now abandoned her studies) had a loving reunion with her during the Christmas vacation (Mina writing in her diary that 'under my care she has changed from a frightened, rebellious child into an independent, reliable girl'). Mina subsequently went to stay with Henrietta at Melcombe Bingham, and there disaster struck. The facts are unclear; but it seems that Henrietta's alcoholic older brother Bobbie made a pass at Mina and, having been rejected, avenged himself by revealing to his father the amorous nature of Mina's friendship with Henrietta. A row ensued, the upshot being that the Judge ordered Mina from his house and forbade his daughter to have anything further to do with her. Henrietta was distraught: she and Mina had planned to spent the summer of 1924 together in London, but although the Judge agreed that Henrietta might accompany him when he went to England on business in May, any future contacts with Mina would have to be secret and furtive.[84]

Tommy remained close to Bunny, who was about to publish his second sucessful novel, *The Man in the Zoo* (jointly dedicated to Mina and Henrietta), and who decided to hold another birthday party in Duncan's studio in March 1924. Possibly to avoid dwelling on the fact that this would be the anniversary of his meeting Henrietta, Tommy asked Bunny whether, as a (typically Bloomsbury) lark, he might disguise himself as a grizzled old beggar offering to tell the fortunes of the guests at the party. 'He would have, he pointed out, the advantage of knowing a great deal about the characters of those whose fortunes he was to tell.' Bunny willingly went along with the imposture, which was highly successful: nobody (not even Garrow) recognised Tommy (who had considerable acting ability), attired in ragged clothes and a filthy white beard, and everyone allowed themselves to be led up to him to discuss their futures. 'Their faces as they emerged were extremely funny. Tommy was an intimate friend of almost every man and woman in the gathering and did not scruple to include either a shattering home-truth or a piece of knowledge which they did not care to have known.' Eventually the beggar departed and soon afterwards Tommy appeared, apologising for being late. When, some days later, the truth leaked out, some of the guests were extremely angry and at least one of them, a beautiful woman, never spoke to Tommy again. Tommy was himself disconcerted not only to hear some of the things his 'customers' had said about him, but also to observe the disdainful manner they adopted when addressing (as they thought) one of the 'lower orders': he told Bunny 'that he could never feel the same again to one handsome young man [probably Angus Davidson] who was a close friend of his ... [who] had almost exaggeratedly good manners when talking to his social equals'.[85]

In the year since he had met them at Bunny's previous party, Tommy had got to know the writer Lytton Strachey (1880–1932) and his companion the artist Dora Carrington (1893–1932). Coming from a large and talented family, and possessing an incisive mind and a biting wit, Lytton was widely regarded as the heart and soul of the Bloomsbury Group. After a slow start in his literary career, he had made a tremendous impact with his irreverent biographical studies *Eminent Victorians* (1918) and *Queen Victoria* (1921), which had brought him fame and fortune. Ungainly and perpetually ailing (though his long beard and searching eyes gave him a strik-ing appearance), he was a masochistic homosexual who derived pleasure from worshipping attractive and assertive young men. However, since 1917 he had been living at Tidmarsh Mill in Berkshire in an unusual but close platonic relationship with the younger and bisexual Carrington. Towards the end of the war they had been joined there by Ralph Partridge, a handsome friend, from Oxford and the Western Front, of Carrington's elder brother Noel; Lytton had fallen in love with Ralph (as to some extent

Tommy with Carrington and Lytton, photographed by Lady Ottoline Morrel at Garsington

had Carrington), and in order to preserve 'the triangle', Carrington had married Ralph in 1921. The *ménage* was further complicated by the fact that Ralph tended to fall in love with other women, and was currently enamoured of Bunny's sister-in-law Frances Marshall, while several other men were in love with Carrington, notably Ralph's wartime friend Gerald Brenan. It is not clear how Tommy's early relations with Lytton and Carrington developed, but Tommy went to stay with them at Tidmarsh on at least a couple of occasions between the summer of 1923 and the spring of 1924, as well as meeting them at other houses such as Garsington;* and they were both taken with him. Early in 1924 Lytton and Ralph bought a bigger house (found by Carrington), Ham Spray in the Wiltshire Downs, but continued to live at Tidmarsh for the rest of that year while extensive work was carried out on the new

* The country house near Oxford of Lady Ottoline Morrell (daughter of a duke, wife of a Liberal MP, and an eminent 'culture vulture'), where she had provided a refuge for the Bloomsberries during the First World War, employing several conscientious objectors among them (including Clive Bell) as farm labourers

property. Tommy was invited to join the house party at Tidmarsh at Whitsun 1924.

Shortly before this party assembled, Henrietta arrived in London with her father. Her reunion with Tommy was, as her biographer puts it, 'awkward'. In the nine months since their parting she had undergone a considerable trauma; such feelings as she had had for him had cooled. She did not even seem particularly keen to see him: Bunny had to do much telephoning to bring about a meeting. She nevertheless agreed to accompany him to Tidmarsh.[86] What possibly neither of them realised was that, at Bunny's thirtieth birthday fifteen months earlier, Carrington no less than Tommy had been smitten by Henrietta. As she wrote to Gerald Brenan at the time: 'I only know her name is Henrietta. She has the face of a Giotto Madonna. She sang exquisite songs with a mandoline … She made such exquisite cocktails that I became completely drunk and almost made love to her in public.'[87] Carrington had not then declared her feelings, but now made up for lost time. At Tidmarsh, Henrietta largely ignored Tommy and embarked on a wild affair with Carrington which would absorb her for the next two months. This caused dismay not just to Tommy but also to Gerald Brenan, who had recently arrived in London from Spain in the hope of resuming his affair with Carrington, as well as to Mina: with a view to a lovers' reunion with Henrietta, Mina had arranged to visit London in June with her brothers, but by the time she got there Henrietta was no more interested in her than in Tommy. Tommy was only able to continue seeing Henrietta by accompanying her to Ham Spray, where they helped Carrington decorate the house and create a garden, and Henrietta carried on her affair with Carrington. Carrington took photographs of Henrietta and Tommy which show them looking uncomfortable together: they have forced smiles on their faces; Henrietta, immaculate in riding habit, almost looks as if she is about to beat Tommy, cowering in a shabby suit, with her crop. Tommy consoled himself by embarking on an affair

Henrietta and Tommy at Ham Spray, June 1924

with Barbara Bagenal,* an artist friend of Carrington who was also helping with the work at Ham Spray. He had a fling too with Mina's brother Lincoln Kirstein, a handsome sixteen-year-old with strong gay inclinations (also helping out at Ham Spray) who was to achieve

---

* Barbara Bagenal (*née* Hiles, [1891–1984]) had been a fellow student of Carrington at the Slade. She was known for her bohemian ways, and had spent part of the First World War living in a tent on Vanessa Bell's lawn. The original Bloomsbury Group member Saxon Sydney-Turner was in love with her, but in 1918 she embarked on a rather 'free' marriage with Nick Bagenal. Her affair with Tommy seems to have continued on and off for a couple of years, Tommy joining her and her husband and children for their family Christmas in 1925. While often thinking her rather silly, Bloomsbury as a whole was fond of 'Little Ba'.

celebrity in the 1930s by founding the New York City Ballet: Lincoln writes in his memoirs that he was infatuated with Tommy and that his greatest delight that summer was to sit with him in his studio watching him draw life models, and that he felt privileged when Tommy, preparing to go to a grand dinner, allowed him to scrub his back while he bathed, and put the studs in his dress shirts.[88]

Meanwhile Tommy had been invited, along with Frank Dobson, to stay that July with Leo Myers at a sixteenth-century castle Myers was renting at Portofino in Italy; and he accepted the invitation after Henrietta had promised to join him in Paris afterwards. (While behaving coolly towards him, she did not reject him; flirtatious by nature, she seems to have done just enough to maintain his passion and sustain his hopes.) He wrote to her from Portofino, mentioning a 'ravishing little American blond' he had met on the train whom she would have found 'distinctly bedworthy', and 'one or two god-like fisher boys' who 'spread their nets where we bathe' and 'pluck the heart-strings a little'.[89] From there he went to stay at another castle, the Fortezza della Brunella at Aulla, owned by his mother's reclusive cousin, the artist Aubrey Waterfield; and he continued to Venice, where some of Dobson's sculpture was being exhibited at the Biennale, and Myers accommodated the party at the Hotel Excelsior on the Lido, which revolted Tommy with its opulent vulgarity. At the end of the month he met Henrietta in Paris, as arranged: we know nothing about this episode, except that Tommy also took the opportunity (possibly in Henrietta's company) to see Yvonne, the French nursemaid of his childhood, who was living near the capital in a lesbian ménage with Louise Falque, a sculptor and aviator who dressed and behaved like a man. Certainly his reunion with Henrietta did nothing either to cool his ardour or rekindle her desire to spend time with him, as soon after their return to England he wrote to her lamenting that the hours he spent thinking about her vastly exceeded 'the few minutes I have now and then in your company'.[90]

In August Henrietta's father, who had gone back to America to attend the Democratic Convention for the coming presidential election, returned to England, together with her brothers, and the four of them left for a week's grouse shooting in Argyll. When they got there, Henrietta received a shock. Her father announced that he had proposed marriage to a respectable but unremarkable widow they all knew in Louisville, Aleen Muldoon Hilliard: she had accepted him, and the wedding would take place at St Margaret's, Westminster on 20 August. Henrietta and her brothers were appalled: they (and others who knew the family, including Mina, Bunny and Tommy) were convinced that this sudden (and doubt-fully suitable) matrimonial project* was principally motivated by a desire on the Judge's part to avenge himself on Henrietta for her coldness towards him in recent years, and her 'unnatural' affairs with Mina and others. Dr Jones, who knew that Henrietta's ambig-uous relationship with her father lay at the heart of her troubled psychology, told Mina that he feared for her stability. Henrietta wrote to Tommy and Carrington asking them to be in London to support her at this terrible time. However, no sooner was the wedding over than Henrietta departed on a motoring tour of France with yet another girlfriend, a red-headed American.[91]

Tommy was in the depths of misery, but kept himself busy by working on busts of Barbara Bagenal (never completed) and Duncan Grant (a bronze cast of which is now in the National Por-trait Gallery). The fact that both he and Carrington had effectively been thrown over by Henrietta drew them together. 'Carrington dear', he wrote to her at the end of September, 'I have little to tell ... I got back to London a week ago yesterday (after a gloomy sojourn with my family) & I saw her [Henrietta] then & spent a heavenly afternoon with her, shopping. I saw her for a minute or two on Saturday... It is a good deal my fault that I have not

* A woman of few social accomplishments, Aleen would be a liability to her husband when, a decade later, he became US Ambassador to London.

Tommy's bust of Duncan

seen more of her. For the past three weeks I have been possessed
of a devil of gloom & fear, so that I have not often answered my
door bell or gone to the telephone ... I have almost decided to try
the Wizard [Ernest] Jones, for a consultation at least ... When I
saw H. she was incredibly beautiful & comforting. I foresee an
autumn of despair however.'[92] Tommy attended a lecture given by
Jones at Oxford, and met him afterwards at a dinner; but on learning that the doctor charged three guineas an hour, and expected
new patients to sign up for at least seventy sessions, he recoiled.

However, after seeking the advice of Lytton's brother James, he went to see Dr Edward Glover, a respected psychoanalyst who was able to help him and whom he consulted intermittently for the rest of his life. (Glover told James that he had diagnosed Tommy as a severe case of 'D.P.' – dual personality:[93] Tommy certainly struck many people as being a 'Jekyll and Hyde' character, and swung between moods of depression and elation.)

Something which provided a welcome distraction for Tommy at this time was that Bunny, following the success of his two novels, decided to give up bookselling to concentrate on writing, and to move, with his pregnant wife and infant son, from their flat in London to a house in the country. Their preference was for a property within reach of Cambridge, where many of their friends (including two of Ray Garnett's brothers) lived, and that October they completed the purchase of Hilton Hall, a Jacobean manor house near Huntingdon, set in three acres of grounds. Tommy volunteered to help Bunny with the move, and they spent a busy couple of days carrying furniture, removing ivy and fetching coal. After their labours, drinking beer before a blazing fire, they decided to found an informal men's dining club which would meet once a month in London and enable them to keep in touch with 'each other and the friends who mattered most' (for Tommy too was thinking of living outside the capital, he was not yet sure where); they called it 'the Cranium Club' after Mr Cranium, the egghead in Thomas Love Peacock's novel *Headlong Hall*.[94] The early membership included a few names particular to Tommy, such as his brother Garrow, Leo Myers, Frank Dobson and Roy Harrod; Bunny's publisher Charles Prentice, business partner Frankie Birrell and brother-in-law Tom Marshall; and some young men they had both quite recently got to know, such as Alec Penrose, Gerald Brenan and Sebastian Sprott. But the bulk of the list was 'Old Bloomsbury' – Lytton Strachey and his brother Oliver; Maynard Keynes; Duncan Grant; Leonard Woolf; Adrian Stephen;

Bertrand Russell; Morgan Forster; Saxon Sydney-Turner; Roger Fry ...[95] It is noteworthy that Tommy and Bunny between them felt that these were the men (a generation older than themselves) whose company and conversation they would most miss if they no longer lived in London (though Tommy cannot then have known any of the 'Bloomsberries' for more than a couple of years). The club survives to this day.

Until the end of the year and into the early months of 1925, Tommy remained obsessed with Henrietta. He continued to bombard her with letters, though these now contained a hint of reproach. Regarding her latest lesbian amours, he wrote on 24 November: 'If only they knew what risks they are running – falling in love with you – they would hang themselves before dinner and die happy. I sometimes wish I had done so.'[96] Carrington invited Tommy and Henrietta to Ham Spray for a night, promising 'cross-dressing theatre, followed by dancing to the gramophone and midnight supper'; Henrietta accepted but never turned up, leaving Carrington and Tommy 'furious and miserable'. Bunny wrote inviting her to come with Tommy for 'an old fashioned Christmas' at Hilton; but she preferred to disappear with a party of American friends to Nice.[97] Before leaving, she did spend some time with Tommy; though as he wrote bitterly to Mina, 'that is her method, to reinforce the shackles before putting a strain on them'.[98] In the new year he wrote to her at her French hotel:

> Will you please marry me when you get back? I am perfectly serious. Please do. I see no objections. It is only this damned hanging about that makes it look difficult. We could have done it March 10, '23 [the day after their first meeting] and never regretted it. There is no project that does not appear especially difficult if one shivers on the brink long enough. Please marry me.[99]

One of Tommy's eagles perched on a gatepost at Melcombe Bingham

He waited in vain for a reply. But still he did not give up. When Gerald Brenan asked Vanessa Bell whether Tommy had been upset by Henrietta's indifference, Vanessa replied:

> Probably. But hardly more upset than he has been in the last six months. I have really fancied sometimes he might be going off his head… He thinks she might marry him. He goes on asking her. She never refuses definitely. But of course she never would.[100]

However, the fact that Henrietta kept no more of Tommy's letters indicates that she retained little further interest in him; and they appear to have seen little more of each other before Henrietta returned to America in May 1925. It only remained for him to complete the stone eagles for the Melcombe Bingham gateposts, which he did later that year: they were shipped out to Kentucky, where they remain to this day. Rather surprisingly, these do not show the birds resplendent with outstretched wings (like the bronze eagle adorning the American Embassy in Grosvenor Square, where Henrietta's father would preside as Ambassador during the mid-1930s), but curled up and hiding their heads, as if miserable in captivity. Perhaps this was intended to be a statement of sorts.

One of the oddest aspects of Tommy's life is that, although he possessed undoubted literary talents, and set much store by his connection with 'Bloomsbury', which largely consisted of dedicated correspondents, he himself was strongly averse to writing letters. The only significant body of his correspondence which has come to light consists of the forty-odd letters which he addressed to Henrietta in 1923-4. But in one of the first of these (28 March 1923), he declares: 'If you knew how I loathe writing, & how few letters I write, you might understand, when you get this, how you disturb me. I never write to anyone except in cases of desperation; this *is* a desperate case.' Soon after her return to America, he wrote to her (2 September 1923): 'I have never wanted to write to anyone before; & I still hate writing. But I can't help trying to get into communication with you somehow.' Writing to her, he usually reveals something of his feelings, past doings and future plans; but letters to others generally reveal the minimum on these or any subjects. Even his letters to so close a friend as Roy Harrod rarely occupy more than a couple of pages, largely taken up with apologies for his inadequacy as a correspondent. How is one to explain this circumstance, so unusual for the period, especially in the case of one possessing so highly developed a gift of self-expression? Possibly, during his adolescence, there had been some incident involving a letter which had put him off the practice for life. But his propensity seems above all to reflect an intense desire for secrecy; a refusal to be pinned down; an inclination to give away as little as possible about himself. This tells us something about him – but does not make things easy for his biographers.

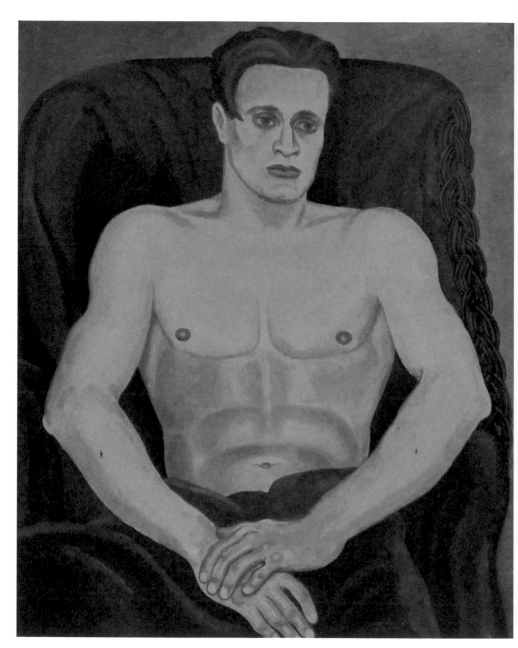

Tommy's portrait by John Banting, 1926

IV

AT THE HEART OF
BLOOMSBURY

1925–1926

Two years after he had encountered 'Bloomsbury' at Bunny Garnett's party in March 1923, Tommy (now twenty-four) had become an established star in their firmament. His bust of Duncan Grant had been completed; although (as with all Tommy's portraits) it did not idealise its subject, it was generally admired. Duncan liked it; bronze casts (costing £40 each) were ordered by the great loves of his life, Maynard Keynes and Bunny.[101] Tommy hoped to follow it with one of Virginia Woolf – 'there is a little thrush like creature called Tomlin who wants to sculpt me', she wrote in her diary just before Christmas 1924[102] – though it was to be another six and a half years before the novelist hesitantly yielded to this project. If Virginia was unsure whether she liked him, her sister Vanessa had few doubts: when their brother and sister-in-law, Adrian and Karin Stephen, gave a party in Fitzroy Square in February 1925, she spent the whole evening talking to Tommy on a sofa.[103] Once a month he got together with the male Bloomsberries at the dinners of the Cranium Club.

During the next couple of years, Tommy's Bloomsbury life was centred on three houses – Ham Spray, Hilton and Charleston.

Lytton, Carrington and Ralph had finally moved into Ham Spray during the late autumn of 1924 (Tommy, accompanied by Barbara Bagenal, staying in the 'completed' house for the first time in mid-December). Although they all wished, in this idyllic new setting, to preserve their unusual household, the relationship between them was under strain, all three parties having found emotional involvement elsewhere. Lytton was infatuated with a (not especially handsome, but clever and bawdy) Cambridge undergraduate named Philip Ritchie, whom Carrington disliked. Carrington still hankered after Henrietta Bingham, whom Lytton disliked; having been thrown over by the American *femme fatale*, she began a hesitant affair with her admirer Gerald Brenan, the grudging nature of which had the effect of driving Brenan (whom Ralph, his wartime friend, was beginning to dislike) almost insane. Ralph, while holding on to his (now largely platonic) marriage with Carrington, was in love with Frances Marshall, and conducting an affair with her both in in London and at Ham Spray: although the tactful and serene Frances was difficult to dislike, she understandably felt uncomfortable at Ham Spray, and occasionally yielded to the advances of another suitor.

This was the explosive emotional mixture in which Tommy became an additional, and highly volatile, element during the years 1925–7. He was loved by both Lytton and Carrington – to the point that they eventually both thought of reconstituting the original 'triangle' with Tommy effectively replacing Ralph as the bisexual resident man. Lytton admired him for his handsome looks, his outwardly breezy personality and his love of intellectual conversation. Whenever he visited London, Tommy was one of the people he most wished to see. Though no correspondence survives which might give an insight into this, it is difficult to believe that Tommy did not engage with Lytton in the mildly sado-masochistic role-playing games which constituted the latter's sex-life.[*] Tommy for his part saw Lytton as a father figure, to whom he might confide his problems. In one of Tommy's few surviving letters to Lytton, dated 15 April 1925, he refers to the mysterious melancholia from

---

[*] An intriguing picture of these games emerges from Lytton's correspondence with another of his late loves – Roger Senhouse.

Ham Spray

which he intermittently suffered: 'I had fondly supposed, some certain point of achievement gained, a man became immune to real depression & possessed a secure reservoir of satisfaction...'[104] Tommy and Carrington felt closely bound both as artists and as fellow sufferers from the siren Henrietta. Tommy's letters to her, though brief and inconsequential, are full of endearments. During 1925, Carrington gradually disengaged herself from Gerald and transferred her romantic interest to Tommy. Their relationship was mostly platonic, but seems to have assumed a physical dimension during the spring of 1926; it aroused the jealousy of both Ralph and Gerald – though by then Ralph had become semi-detached from Ham Spray, generally only going there at weekends and living during the week with Frances in a Bloomsbury flat.*

There are accounts of Tommy during this period in the memoirs of those two peripheral members of the Ham Spray set-up, Frances and Gerald. Though she gave him the benefit of the doubt, Frances saw Tommy as a Jekyll-and-Hyde character.

* Ralph certainly showed extraordinary generosity and patience in this situation, seeing that he was the legal owner of Ham Spray – he had shared the cost of it with Lytton, and it was registered in his name.

...Stephen Tomlin was a case of dual personality. One side of his character was creatively gifted, charming and sensitive; the other was dominated by a destructive impulse (fuelled perhaps by deeply neurotic despair) whose effect was that he couldn't see two people happy together without being impelled to intervene and take one away, leaving the other bereft. Or it would take the form of a direct bid for power over others – whether male or female – which he was well-equipped to exert. The sequel would be a fit of suicidal depression or guilt-feelings. The two sides of his personality were fused together ... by an excellent brain inherited from his father the judge, shown in his enjoyment of arguments... He broke several hearts, but certainly gave more pleasure than the reverse and had many loyal friends; if one could forget his dark side he was an interesting, even enchanting companion. Personally I did forget it most of the time, though when he switched on the charm for my benefit I found it unconvincing; but to Ralph the destructive side was anathema, and when Tommy revealed it he reacted with irritation, even dislike.[105]

Gerald's account is interesting as some of it might well apply to Brenan himself, who was deeply neurotic and (though almost a decade older than Tommy) had produced little of value as a writer by this time (though he would live to an old age and do some impressive work later on).

I always felt that he was more of a literary man than of an artist, in spite of the fact that chiseling stone seemed to fulfil some need in his nature... He could talk to anyone, pouring out a flood of ideas, good bad and indifferent but always stimulating. For talking was his link with others. He could not bear to be alone, but clung to other people, asserting himself vigorously in their company and yet all the time dependent, lonely, demanding friendship and affection. One felt something chaotic and unhappy under his self-confident air and one also felt that his nature held depths and potentialities that were not shared by the other young men one met in Bloombury circles. Yet he was spineless and lacking in direction… A character from a Russian novel perhaps. One felt his imaginative gifts yet knew that they would come to nothing.[106]

Both Frances and Gerald mention Tommy's bisexuality; but while Gerald is dismissive of his looks ('though hardly good looking enough to attract men he often had a great effect on women'), Frances found him attractive: 'He had the striking profile of a Roman emperor on a coin, fair straight hair brushed back from a fine forehead, a pale face and grey eyes.'

Tommy remained close to Bunny and was a frequent guest at Hilton, where he helped with the work which remained to be done on the house and garden, making his mark by planting a chestnut

Bunny and Tommy at Hilton

tree. He got on well with Ray Garnett, being one of Bunny's few romantic attachments towards whom she felt no jealousy. (On the other hand, Bunny himself displayed some jealousy when, in 1926–7, Ray had an affair with Tommy's brother Garrow.[107]) Bunny dedicated to Tommy his fourth novel *Go She Must!*, published in 1927, which dealt (very delicately, owing to the law) with the theme of bisexuality. A great friend of both Tommy and Bunny was Alec Penrose (1896–1950), who had come into their lives when, as a Cambridge postgraduate student, he was (on Frankie Birrell's recommendation) appointed tutor to the teenage brothers of Mina Kirstein during the summer of 1923. He was an attractive and gifted man, but suffered from psychological problems owing to a domineering mother, and was given to rages against the modern world. This endeared him to Tommy, who wrote to Carrington in September 1924: 'I *am* glad you liked Alec. He is much nicer than most people.' Bunny and Tommy also befriended Alec's equally gifted younger brothers Lionel (a scientist), Roland (an artist) and Bernard (known as 'Beakus', a yachtsman); but their favourite was Alec, and they were delighted when, in 1925, Alec (who had substantial private means) bought a house in the next village to Hilton. There were frequent joint house-parties at which Tommy, Garrow and Frankie stayed with Bunny or Alec, and they all got together to go on excursions, or to visit Cambridge, where their many friends included Maynard Keynes (Fellow and Bursar of King's College), the architecture don Geoffrey Webb (known as 'Wobb'), and the brilliant and beautiful student actor George 'Dadie' Rylands.

As a friend of Duncan, Tommy was always welcome at Charleston (though Duncan, no great talker, sometimes found himself 'befuddled' by Tommy's conversation[108]). The set-up there was not dissimilar to Ham Spray: as in the case of Carrington and Lytton, Vanessa was in love with Duncan, contented herself with a platonic relationship and accepted his male lovers (including Tommy); meanwhile she preserved the appearances of her marriage to Clive (as Carrington did with Ralph), while Clive spent most of his time with his mistress Mary Hutchinson (as Ralph did with Frances). One difference was that Clive and Vanessa had two sons, Julian and Quentin, who were sixteen and fourteen at the beginning of 1925: Quentin later recalled that they adored the visits of Tommy, who being something of a perpetual adolescent was the ideal playmate for their games and flights of fancy.[109] (Their little sister Angelica, as was then known to very few, was in fact the love-child of Duncan.) 'It has been most agreeable here, with Clive, Vanessa and Duncan as hosts and Tommy as a fellow guest', wrote Lytton to Roger Senhouse while staying there in September 1926. 'As you may imagine in such company there has been no deficiency in conversation. We totter to bed at two o'clock in the morning, having ranged at large over the characters of our friends and the constitution of the universe, and still uncertain as to the value of representation in art.'[110] Charleston was close to two other rural Bloomsbury households, Leonard and Virginia Woolf at Rodmell

Tommy and Lytton photographed by Vanessa Bell at Charleston, September 1926: on the left Clive Bell is holding his presumed daughter Angelica

(Tommy went on to stay with them after his visit to Charleston in September 1926) and Maynard Keynes and Lydia Lopokova at Tilton. In August 1925 Maynard and Lydia surprised the Bloomsbury world by marrying, Lydia having finally obtained an annulment of her previous marriage. The older Bloomsberries were dismissive of Lydia, who spoke English imperfectly and could not engage in intellectual chat; they also believed that Maynard had made a mistake in marrying her, that he would soon tire of her and return to his homosexual ways. They were misguided on all counts: Lydia was extremely intelligent in her fashion, and devoted to Maynard; and he was genuinely in love with her, to the extent that he had, during the previous two years, put his gay life behind him. Unlike their elders, Bunny and Tommy always seem to have liked and seen the point of Lydia.[111]

Amateur dramatics were a feature of Bloomsbury house-parties, and Tommy, who might have made a career in the theatre, enthusiastically participated in these. In 1913 Lytton had written a melodramatic play, *Son of Heaven*, set in the Chinese imperial palace during the Boxer Rising of 1900; when, thanks to his subsequent celebrity, this received two London performances for charity in July 1925, Tommy played the role of the Executioner. The production was directed by Alec Penrose, with sets by Duncan Grant, costumes by Carrington, music by William Walton and a programme designed by Vanessa Bell; while a professional leading lady was engaged to play the principal role of the Dowager Empress, most of the other parts were taken by Bloomsberries, including Ralph, Gerald, and several of Lytton's relations (though Lytton himself refused to have anything to do with it, going abroad before it took place). It was an enjoyable shambles and inspired several ironical reviews.[112] Tommy himself wrote several plays, some of which received a performance: writing to Bunny years later, Sylvia recalled one of these, entitled *Tom-Tit-Tot*, performed in the garden of a friend of Tommy in Suffolk, in which her role was to strike a large gong.[113] After their marriage, Keynes and Lydia gave parties at their house in Gordon Square which included theatrical revues, for which Tommy, having a gift for comic versification, was in demand as a song-writer. The most memorable of these was inspired by a criminal case involving an eccentric Sussex landowner, Mr Hayley Morriss of Pippingford Park, Uckfield (not far from Charleston), who during the autumn of 1925 was sentenced to two years' hard labour for seducing under-age girls.* In the revue, entitled *Don't be Frightened, or Pippington Park*, 'Clarissa' (i.e. Vanessa, played by Desmond MacCarthy's wife Molly who could not have looked less like her) is abducted from 'Georgetown' (i.e. Charleston) by Morriss (played by Tommy), who lures her into his clutches by offering her a Cézanne and a Giotto. A ballet of artists featured Duncan, Sickert and Roger Fry, while a chorus of female beauties consisted of Angus Davidson, his brother Douglas and Dadie Rylands in drag. Tommy's songs included 'Take me Back to Dear Old Bloomsbury', and the performance ended with the company performing 'the Keynes-Keynes' (i.e. a can-can).[114]

Tommy was now receiving recognition as an artist. The November 1925 issue of London *Vogue* hailed him as 'one of the most promising sculptors of the younger generation', mentioning his 'great gift' for portraiture. Around this time, Tommy gave up the studio in Fulham which he had been renting since 1923 and moved to another in Hampstead, next to the Heath and across the road from the Bull and Bush pub. Then as now, Hampstead Heath was notorious for nocturnal homosexual prowlings; and when Tommy writes from the studio (in a letter to Julia Strachey of September 1926 quoted in the next chapter) that he stayed up late most nights engaging in 'unprofitable' habits which left him feeling 'tired and

---

* A few years later, two of those attending the revue – Ralph Partridge and Frances Marshall – would get to know Morriss, by then released from prison, and concluded that he had been the victim of a grave miscarriage of justice (Frances Partridge, *Memories*, pp. 180–7).

Boris Anrep's mosaic 'Art' in the West Vestibule of the National Gallery

disgusted' next day, one wonders whether he may be alluding to such activities. The studio belonged to Boris Anrep (1883–1969), an exuberant Russian mosaicist who was an old friend of Lytton. (Boris's American wife Helen had recently left him for Roger Fry, after which Boris mostly lived and worked in Paris – hence his having a London studio to let.) In 1926 Boris was commissioned to do a series of mosaics for the vestibule of the National Gallery (which remain in place to this day); one of the tableaux, entitled 'Art', shows a muscular, auburn-haired sculptor at work, clearly inspired by Tommy. Although Tommy himself evidently produced quite a lot of sculpture in 1925 (some of which was exhibited at the Ruskin Galleries in March 1926), not much seems to have

Boris Anrep

survived: apart from the bust of Duncan, we know of only two other portraits completed that year – the subjects being Tommy's sister Joan Trower, and Eddy Sackville-West.

Eddy (1901–65) was a few months younger than Tommy, and an only son. His father was a general; his uncle Lionel, 3rd Baron Sackville, was ancestral owner of Knole in Kent, one of the greatest houses of England. As Lionel had no sons, the title and the Knole estate were due to pass to Eddy's father and then to Eddy.* (Lionel did, however, have a daughter, the novelist and poet Vita Sackville-West, who was married to the homosexual diplomat and writer Harold Nicolson, but who since 1923 had been conducting a largely platonic lesbian relationship with Virginia Woolf, who used her as the inspiration for her novel *Orlando*.) Eddy's mother's family, the Bells, were old Kentish gentry from the Canterbury area, much like (and probably acquainted with) the Tomlins. Eddy was a delicate boy, who spent his childhood being tortured by a succession of

* Eddy's father became Lord Sackville in 1928, Eddy himself in 1962. Knole (though it remains the family home to this day) was acquired by the National Trust in 1946.

Tommy's bust of Eddy Sackville-West, 1925: visiting Knole in September 1926, Lytton wrote to Roger Senhouse that 'the one work of art I really liked was by – who do you think? – Tommy! – a head of Eddy, in lead – full of finesse and charm'

illness, acquiring a taste for suffering. He was clever and gifted, showing a precocious interest in both music and literature. Like Tommy, he was distant from his father but close to his mother: he suffered greatly from her death when he was nineteen, and his father's subsequent marriage to an American actress. He developed a self-centered and neurotic personality, though he possessed some charm and made many friends both at Eton and Oxford, most of them aesthetes like himself. Though quite distinguished-looking in his frail way, he had a disastrous tendency to develop crushes on handsome adonises who, while amused by his company, treated him with breezy contempt. He had made himself miserable (a condition he rather enjoyed) by falling in love (platonically) with a hearty boy called Snagge at Eton, and (erotically) with a muscular sportsman called McDougal at Oxford. He relieved his feelings by writing a novel inspired by these infatuations, published in 1926 as *The Ruin*, and in 1924 visited Germany to consult a doctor who he hoped would cure him of his tendencies through psychoanalysis.[115]

It is not known how Tommy and Eddy first met. Possibly they had known each other in childhood through Kentish connections; possibly the link was through Bloomsbury (as an Oxford undergraduate Eddy had visited Garsington and got to know the Bells, the Woolfs and Lytton Strachey), or through Roy Harrod (who became a don at Christ Church, Eddy's college, in 1922). But they certainly knew each other by the end of 1924, as Eddy was one of the original members of the Cranium Club founded by Tommy and Bunny in November that year (and it seems likely that his name was proposed by Tommy rather than Bunny). At all events, towards the end of 1925 Tommy, who had been working on a bust of Eddy, succeeded Snagge and McDougal as Eddy's latest self-torturing infatuation. 'Did you know that Eddy S.-W. is desperately in love with Tommy like everyone else?', wrote Vanessa to Duncan on 27 December.[116] In the new year, an encounter between them brought Eddy to the verge of a nervous breakdown; he fled to seek solace with his cousin Vita, who wrote to Virginia Woolf on 8 January 1926: 'He limped into my room, wasted away to a ghost, and limped out again, back to bed. He had had a visit from the devastating Tomlin.'[117] Curiously, at that same moment Tommy was unburdening himself to Virginia, who wrote to Vita: 'I had an interview with the devastation of all hearts, Stephen Tomlin, who is flying, like Daphne,* pursued by his lovers, to a refuge in the outskirts of London where no one shall follow him, for he says he is now half crazy: wishing to love, and to give, accepting every [presumably sexual] invitation, and then finding, what appals him, that people love him in return. I found him rather an interesting object ... in that he resembles me ... in his myriad minded

---

* A nymph in classical mythology, who avoided the unwanted attentions of the god Apollo by turning herself into a laurel tree.

innumerable curiosity about others…'[118] (But she did not share in the physical admiration of him, adding that, though he was 'sprightly as an elf', she found him 'misshapen as a Woodpecker'.)[119]

Despite the mutual anguish to which the affair of Tommy and Eddy had led, they seem to have resumed it not long afterwards. Early in 1926, as the heir to Knole, Eddy was given a set of private apartments there, and began a visitors book in which Tommy's name features in 1926–7. So strongly was Eddy under Tommy's spell that he meekly submitted when Tommy suggested they go hiking across the downs with knapsacks, refreshing themselves in pubs – an activity far from Eddy's usual routine. Having sat to Tommy for a bust in 1925, Eddy had him sit the following year for a portrait to John Banting, the striking bare-chested portrait which adorns the cover of this book. Banting, an early British Surrealist, was the same age as Eddy and Tommy. The son of a bookbinder, he had studied art in Paris while working as a life model. In 1925 he took a studio near Duncan's and Vanessa's in Fitzroy Street, where he painted Eddy's portrait that year. Eddy mentions him (along with Tommy) in a list of his lovers;[120] and that Banting's relations with Tommy also went beyond those of artist and sitter is suggested by a letter he wrote to Bunny Garnett from the South of France during the 1930s, alluding to 'a short interlude with a tough which ended with his robbing me … he had a certain something of Tommy about him'.[121] Eddy cherished Banting's portrait of Tommy for the rest of his life, and as late as 1953 was reminded of Tommy by the breezy adonis in Mary Renault's homosexual novel *The Charioteer*.[122] Certainly Tommy, while he was alive, did not cease to flutter Eddy's heart-strings: in a sporadic diary, Eddy 'remembered with horror' an occasion when he lay ill in hospital awaiting a visit from Tommy, when the door opened to admit not Tommy but his brother Garrow. 'I shall never forget how I arranged my face … so that G. should not see [the disappointment]. That was real suffering, and as such deserved to be turned into art.'[123]

John Banting

At some point during 1925 or 1926 Tommy broke off relations with one of his oldest friends – Sylvia Townsend Warner, whom he had known since his arrival at Harrow (where her father was the universally loved history master) in 1914. Both the precise circumstances of the episode and its date are difficult to establish, as Sylvia was so traumatised by it that she seems eventually to have destroyed not only all letters she had received from Tommy, but most other correspondence or diaries in her possession which alluded to their friendship.* (Fortunately she still had some of this material to hand, and quoted from it, when, during the 1930s, she wrote an account of

* In 2012, Susan Fox was assured by the archivist at the Dorset County Museum, which holds Sylvia's papers, that they contained no material relating to or even mentioning Tommy. The authors have been unable to consult the archives themselves as they are currently closed to researchers.

her early contacts with Theo Powys and Chaldon Herring.) What
is clear is that Tommy not only found her physically unattractive
but, compared to his Bloomsbury friends, socially and intellectually
dull; and he increasingly resented her demands on his time and
attention, later telling Bunny that 'the strain of her company grew
worse every year'.[124] Sylvia, however, who had long been in love
with him, was unable to keep away; and eventually Tommy (probably in his cups) turned on her in an outburst in which he expressed

Tommy's caricature of Sylvia

his feelings of repulsion towards her with some brutality. The result (in the words of Sylvia's biographer) was 'an irrevocable, deeply wounding break'.[125] It was no doubt ungrateful of him to behave in this way, for Sylvia had not only provided him with a refuge during the confused period following his departure from Oxford in 1919, but down the years had offered a shoulder for him to cry on during his not infrequent moments of black depression. But it was indicative of his ruthless side that he made no attempt to mend the relationship once the break had occurred – despite the fact that Sylvia remained a friend of Bea Howe,* Bunny Garnett, Theo Powys and other people with whom Tommy continued to associate, and that she eventually went to live in Chaldon, which he continued to visit. Sylvia subsequently wrote much poetry on the theme of love betrayed, which Tommy's rejection of her doubtless inspired; while Tommy did a cruel caricature of her, which ended up in the possession of Bunny. It took her some years to get over the episode, though she was consoled by her growing success as a woman of letters (she had three novels and three volumes of short stories published during the years 1926–30), and by her lesbian 'marriage' (from 1930) to the young poet Valentine Ackland, another woman emotionally damaged by romantic disappointments.

* Bea, who remained fond of Sylvia, found it hard to forgive Tommy. She later wrote that he 'took from Sylvia's generosity far more than he was prepared to give in return', and that his departure 'affected her deeply, wounding her pride and creating a wide gap in her life' (Foreword to *For Sylvia* by Valentine Ackland [1985], p. 8). In speaking to Sylvia's biographer Claire Harman, and other writers, she put the blackest construction on his behaviour.

Tommy's portrait by Carrington, 1926

V

JULIA

1926–1927

Between May and September 1926 Tommy spent most of his time at Ham Spray. He designed two pieces of statuary for the garden – a weather vane in the form of 'two mermaids in an amatory embrace',[126] and a 'very classical and elegant' statue of 'a nymph [Balanis] of the ilex tree with a cornucopia of fruit',[127] which evoked much admiration when, during the autumn, it was cast in lead and installed beneath the Ham Spray ilex. He wrote a lengthy poem about Ham Spray and its inhabitants, a pastiche of Andrew Marvell's *Upon Appleton House*,* to which Lytton refers delightedly in a letter,[128] but of which, sadly, no copy has been found. During those months, Tommy drew close to Carrington: their relationship was more spiritual than carnal, though it certainly expressed itself sexually on occasion. She painted his portrait, and they went for long noctural walks in the woods to hear the nightingale, which when reported to Gerald drove him mad with jealousy. According to Gerald's memoirs, Tommy was at this time 'being tried out as a substitute for Ralph, to form the third leg of the tripod'.[129] Lytton (who since the end of 1925 had been engaged in writing the last and most intriguing of his books, *Elizabeth and Essex*, in which he used the well-known historical tale as a vehicle for exploring his own

---

* A long poem of ninety-six stanzas, containing much sexual innuendo and biblical allusion, written in 1651 in praise of the country house near York of Marvell's patron Lord Fairfax – which was originally a nunnery, acquired in the early sixteenth century by Fairfax's ancestor who had fallen in love with one of the novices.

feelings) was certainly delighted by Tommy's company and conversation, as well as presumably by his assistance in sexual matters.
However, during August Lytton fell in love with the Old Etonian
Roger Senhouse, a Cambridge friend of Philip Ritchie whom
he had known (though not intimately) for more than a year;* his
feelings were to some extent reciprocated, and so long as the affair
continued, Tommy occupied a subordinate place in the affections
of Lytton, who commissioned him to do a bust of Roger.

Also much in evidence at Ham Spray that summer were three
other members of the Strachey family – Lytton's younger brother,
the psychoanalyst James; James's American-born wife Alix (also
a psychoanalyst); and Lytton's and James's niece Julia, daughter of
their older brother Oliver. Something must be said about Julia,
who was to marry Tommy.

Oliver (1874–1960) was six years older than Lytton, though he
would survive him by almost thirty years. He was intellectually
outstanding, as he would prove as a government codebreaker in
two world wars, but lazy and self-indulgent. After Eton and Bal-
liol he hoped to become a concert pianist; when he turned out to
lack the necessary talent, he accepted a job with the Indian railway
company of which his father had been chairman, spending a dozen
years in Allahabad. There he met and married a young German-
Swiss woman, Ruby Mayer; Julia, their only child, was born in
August 1901. Julia's earliest years in India were happy, but at the age
of six she experienced a succession of shocks. She sailed for Europe
with her mother; Ruby disembarked at Rome, while Julia, accompanied by a nurse, continued alone to England. Apart from a few
embarrassed contacts in the 1930s, Julia would never see or hear
from her mother again. (Ruby had in fact gone to Rome to give
birth to an illegitimate child; having done so she was divorced by
Oliver, and proceeded to remarry several times.) Having loved the

---

* Senhouse was then twenty-eight, three years older than Tommy; Lytton was
forty-seven.

Tommy with his
statue 'Balanis' in
the grounds of Ham
Spray, with Julia
Strachey (who may
have been the model
for the statue's head)
on his right and
Carrington on his
left

colour, heat and clamour of India, and been smothered with affection by her parents and their servants, Julia found herself being brought up amid the fog and ice of a London winter by a dour Scotch nanny in the silent nursery of the gloomy Kensington house of her father's much older sister, the laconic Elinor Rendel: she was traumatised both by the unwelcome change in her surroundings and by the sudden, total and inexplicable disappearance of her mother, the person she had loved best in the world.

Julia endured this hated environment for three years until she was sent away to boarding school aged nine. For a moment, her fortunes seemed to take a benign turn. In 1911 her father retired from his job in India, returned to England, and married a family

friend, the suffragette Ray Costelloe. Ray's mother Mary Berenson, married *en secondes noces* to the famous Florence-based art
historian Bernard Berenson, was the eldest of three children who
had inherited an American glass fortune, the others being the
writer Logan Pearsall Smith and Alys Russell, recently deserted
wife of the philosopher Bertrand Russell. That summer these three
glamorous and cultured siblings rented Iffley Court, a house on
the Thames, to which they invited a large party of friends and
relations. Julia was included, and was enchanted.

> As I listened to them all teasing each other, making outrageous
> allegations, contradicting and doing battle with each other, and
> laughing all the while, I felt I had been … lifted out of the dark
> ages, out of … the old Scottish nursery at Melbury Road, and
> also out of [her boarding school] with its terrifying German
> headmistress … I had been let out from prison into the mellow
> Pagan airs of this free Olympus, where these over-life-size gods
> and godesses … were discovered at play. I heard laughter, joy
> and revelry, things I had not encountered since I had left my
> Indian home.

Following this experience, Julia was quite pleased to learn that she
would henceforth be living not with Oliver and Ray (who would
remain relative strangers to her), but with Ray's bachelor uncle
Logan and childless aunt Alys, who lived together first at Ford
Place, a romantic Elizabethan house near Arundel, later in St
Leonard's Terrace, Chelsea. However, although life in this opulent
household was educational, and brought her into contact with
many charming visitors, it proved to be almost as joyless and
unnerving as her earlier life with Aunt Elinor. Logan was a manic
depressive, who sparkled at his weekend house-parties but was
otherwise a creepy, lifeless presence; Alys (or 'Aunt Loo', as she
was known), though devoted to good works, was an eccentric,
puritanical woman incapable of either giving or receiving affection.

They both made it clear that they had 'adopted' Julia out of charity rather than affection, and that she was a disappointment to them, as they wanted a cheerful, outgoing child, whereas she tended to be morose and self-absorbed.

Like Tommy, Julia was at boarding school during the First World War – in her case Bedales in Hampshire, the 'liberal' co-educational school founded in 1899 (chosen for her, and the fees paid, by Alys). Her friends there included Frances Marshall, future sister-in-law of Bunny Garnett and lover (eventually wife) of Ralph Partridge. Though intelligent, she was a difficult girl, and did not have the discipline to learn systematically. She developed into a boyishly handsome young woman with long legs and a fine figure, but was notoriously vague and disorganised. After the war, she plunged into Bloomsbury social life. (She had a double family connection – Lytton and James were her uncles; and Karin Costelloe, sister of her stepmother Ray, had married Adrian Stephen, brother of Vanessa and Virginia.) She loved going to parties, and enjoyed conversation, to which she brought a critical if unformed mind. She adored visiting the luxurious and sophisticated milieu of Bernard and Mary Berenson in Florence. She continued to live with Logan and Alys at St Leonard's Terrace until she was twenty, when they asked her to leave, giving her a weekly allowance of £3 towards her future keep. She moved into lodgings with her friend Hester Chapman (later a romantic novelist), and intermittently worked (though owing to her unpunctuality no job ever lasted long) as a commercial artist and as a fashion model. For eighteen months she lodged in the house in Gordon Square of her father and stepmother (who now had two young children of their own), an arrangement which proved uncomfortable. She had many male admirers; and although, following her loveless childhood, she yearned for love and affection, her attitude towards them was ambivalent. At least two of the men on whom she developed 'crushes' were homosexual – the flamboyant Eddie Gathorne-Hardy, brother of Lord Cranbrook (and the model for 'Miles Malpractice', the outrageous 'queer' in Evelyn Waugh's novel *Vile Bodies*), and Cecil Pinsent, a handsome architect and garden designer working at the Berensons' villa outside Florence. The relation to whom she felt closest was her uncle James Strachey, who seems to have had a (not entirely unwelcome) incestuous passion for her; it was probably James and Alix who first brought her to Ham Spray, where the three of them were (along with Tommy) in semi-permanent residence during the summer of 1926.

The appearance of Julia added a further exotic element to the emotional mix at Ham Spray. Lytton thought her 'a strange bird but with habits unlike any other bird'.[130] Carrington found her alluring, but considered her untouchable: it was 'maddening', she

Tommy at Ham Spray with Carrington (left), Julia (standing centre) and Barbara Bagenal (crouching)

wrote to Gerald, 'to have (or rather not "have") a lily white lady with Chinese eyes & arms of purest milk sleeping night after night in my house, & there's nothing to be done but admire her from a distance, & steal distracted kisses under cover of saying goodnight'.[131] Meanwhile Julia received amorous attentions from James, while Tommy worked on a bust of – and probably also slept with – James's wife Alix. However, to most onlookers, Tommy and Julia – who were the same age (Julia the younger by five months), both physically attractive, and whose young lives had both been wracked, one way or another, with emotional trauma – seemed a perfect pair; and Carrington, one of life's matchmakers, encouraged their affair. (They had already known each other for at least a year, having both acted in Lytton's *Son of Heaven* in July 1925; and Tommy knew her father, with whom he played piano duets, through the Cranium Club.) After Lytton became absorbed in Roger that August, Tommy drew closer to Julia – possibly she reminded him of that other luscious but confused woman with whom he had recently been besotted, Henrietta. At all events, their intimacy developed rapidly; for by the end of the summer Tommy had apparently decided that she might somehow prove his salvation. In September, while she was staying in the country, he wrote her a 'damned gloomy' letter from his Hampstead studio, mentioning his hobnobbing with Alec, Eddy, John Banting, Lytton and her father Oliver, and continuing:

> And so I go on staying up late every night, disturbed by vague unprofitable emotions, in the morning tired & disgusted & unable to work well. But I think constantly of you; often very loose thoughts, but also with love & with great pleasure. No, sometimes, I confess, with pain, but not often. I want you to be with me, to laugh with you and at you. Darling, won't you snatch a brand from the burning,* as we say in Low Church

---

* A biblical allusion (from Zecharia 3:2), meaning to save a soul from damnation.

circles? My dearest creature ... I love you very much... I send
you kisses, if you'll have them. God bless you.[132]

By the time they spent Christmas 1926 at Ham Spray they had
decided to live together in Paris over the winter in what was
described as a 'trial marriage'. That this project was undertaken in
a spirit of escape rather than amatory bliss is suggested by a letter
written by Julia to Carrington (who had become her confidante)
on 2 December.

Really, the news about going to France ... has gone *too* far.
Frances says to Ralph – 'Heard the latest? Julia & Tommy are
off to settle down in Paris!' Ralph tells everyone he meets, &
suppose it *shouldn't* come off after all?... Pippa [her maiden

Julia in the foreground; in the background (left to right) Lytton,
Tommy, St John Hutchinson and Julia's father Oliver Strachey

aunt Philippa Strachey] goes round with ashen face saying
'Tommy *must* be made to marry poor little Julia, it's *too* awful
– she'll frighten all the dukes & millionaires away if she
becomes a loose woman like this.' ... James's state of mind fills
me with utter depression. He has so much more of a feeling for
me than Tommy does, obviously. I feel a loathsome brute not
to respond wholeheartedly to such affection.[133]

From a letter of Vanessa to Duncan we learn that Oliver (not that
he had ever been much of a father to Julia) shared his sister's
concern about what he described as Julia's 'elopement' with Tommy;
and also that there had been a recent resumption of the old love
affair between Tommy and his Harrow friend Angus Davidson,
which had plunged the latter into a state of despair[134] – just as
Julia saw the Paris experiment as an escape from James, so Tommy
may have seen it as an escape from Angus.

Tommy and Julia lived together in Paris from January to May
1927. What little we know of their life there comes mostly from
Julia's letters to Carrington. They stayed at the Hotel Victoria in

Angus Davidson, who conceived a passion for Tommy at Harrow and
remained in love with him a decade later

the Boulevard St-Michel, where Angus (who followed them to the French capital) called on them 'with a large bouquet of flowers for me and a bottle of Phenacetin for Tommy'.* (Phenacetin is a strong pain-killer, now universally banned, then commonly used by cocaine addicts to 'cut' their drug.) They also rented a studio in rue Turgot, Montmartre, with french windows giving onto a small balcony and a splendid view of the rooftops, but life was so cheap thanks to the weak franc that they kept on their hotel bedroom: on their combined income of £6 a week (Julia getting £3 from Alys and Tommy the same from his father, the whole amounting to about £350 in the values of 2019) they were able to live comfortably, a four course meal with wine and coffee costing the equivalent of two shillings. They went out to dine every evening at 7.30 and rarely returned before midnight: Julia refers, perhaps in jest, to Tommy's 'hissing mob of lovers' on the *quai* outside the restaurant. Tommy enrolled at an art school, where he spent most of his days. They saw many people they knew, including Julian Bell, Roland Penrose, Boris Anrep and the aesthete Harold Acton. Julia wrote to Carrington that 'Tommy seems fairly cheerful – though he is depressed about his sculpture & thinks that his course of analysis ruined any talent he had for it'; he often spoke of Ham Spray, saying that 'the happiest times of his life have been spent there with you & Lytton'. To Roy Harrod Tommy wrote: 'Here I study Art: rather vague & I suspect unprofitable. However I am at a loss in my work & get some comfort from the idea that I am doing something practical about it… I am as happy as I can ever expect to be nowadays, but I hate this city.'

At Easter they visited the *Côte d'Azur* to stay with Clive, Vanessa and Duncan who were renting the Villa Corsica, Cassis with its fine view of the harbour, Vanessa's sister Virginia, Tommy's

* 'Poor Angus, like a dull obsessed woman, has gone scrambling over to Paris to "feast his eyes for one brief moment" on Tommy. Such lack of proper pride is pitiful to see.' (Eddy Sackville-West to Clive Bell, 14 April 1927 [Boston College archives].)

Vanessa and Duncan at Cassis

brother Garrow and John Banting also joining the party. Virginia afterwards wrote to Vanessa: 'Did Tommie [*sic*] and Julia confide in you [about how they were getting on]? How anyone can think him attractive physically passes me. But I am not a judge of the manly form, I suppose. He reminds me of George's* opera hat – the thing he carried under his arm to make him look diplomatic.'[135] Vanessa replied: 'Tommy and Julia did not confide in me. All I heard was from Douglas [Davidson, brother of Angus], who said they seemed to get on quite well as man and wife. They shared a room and bed … and I suppose Julia finds Tommy more attractive

* Their half-brother (Sir) George Duckworth (1868–1934), civil servant.

Tommy and Garrow,
photographed by
John Banting, off
for a swim at Cassis

than you do. They are a slightly curious couple, however. I don't think either is in love with the other, but perhaps they supply wants in each other. I should find either horribly uncomfortable to live with.'[136]

There followed an odd irony. Since his late teens, Tommy had (to quote Duncan) been leading 'a very rackety life'. He had had innumerable sexual encounters with both men and women, some in the nature of single escapades, others 'affairs' lasting days, weeks or months. But all had (presumably) been conducted with reasonable discretion, behind closed doors. There had (so far as is known) been no scandals. His affair with Julia in Paris represented, one might have thought, a fairly respectable episode in his life, a prolonged period of relative monogamy. Yet it was conducted in public, in that they lived together in a hotel, and went about as a couple. News of it was therefore calculated to alarm his highly respectable parents. In March 1927 Tommy's younger and favourite sister Helen, then in her second year as an undergraduate at Somerville College, Oxford, visited Paris and spent an enjoyable time with Tommy and Julia (who found her, as she reported to Carrington, 'a perfect peach'). Helen knew better than to tell her parents about the *ménage*; but she innocently mentioned it to her older sister Joan Trower, who had long regarded Tommy's mode of life with some disapproval, and who suggested to their mother that Tommy had compromised Helen by inviting her 'to dine with him and his mistress'.[137] Tommy (who found it hard to forgive Joan) subsequently found himself in the absurd position of having to marry Julia or risk losing the modest family allowance on which he depended. (As noted above, even Julia's fairly bohemian father and aunt had been slightly shocked at the idea of Tommy and Julia living together without being married. It was all a matter of appearances.)

But why not marry her? She seemed willing; the experiment of living with her had been reasonably successful; it would make Tommy the nephew-in-law of his beloved Lytton; and it would be a Bloomsbury marriage, no more inhibiting to his future life than Clive's marriage to Vanessa, Bunny's to Ray or Ralph's to Carrington. Before leaving England, Tommy had arranged to rent a cottage in Swallowcliffe, Wiltshire (a village about forty miles from Ham Spray), which might serve as their matrimonial home.

While musing on the matter, Tommy received desperate appeals from Lytton, who was in the depths of misery, having received a letter from Roger Senhouse which he interpreted as breaking off their affair. They had had a successful holiday in Rome in the new year; but at the end of March Roger wrote to him that, fond of Lytton though he was, he was starting to feel overwhelmed by his attentions, and required a period of separation. This was kindly meant, and did not imply a total rupture; but Lytton had become so dependent on Roger that he found his emotional universe shattered. On the verge of a breakdown, he sought the support of his friends; and Tommy (returning to England in May) was one of two friends – the other was Dadie Rylands – whose ministrations helped restore his fragile equilibrium. Tommy's solicitude was not entirely disinterested. Now that Roger was (at least temporarily) out of the picture, and Tommy was again looked upon as one of the mainstays of Ham Spray, it occurred to him that Lytton might help provide the financial support which his family was threatening to cut off. As Tommy wrote to Lytton on 21 May:

> I've been thinking over your very kind offer of a loan and as the family appear to be thoroughly on the war path, I feel very inclined to accept... It looks as if there is going to be a bad smash. I gather the cat is out of the bag* & my married sister, a savage woman, is opening a campaign. They are all behaving in a way that you who do not know them could not credit. They begin to close on me with the strangest antics, like dancing cannibals; they are jungle fowl. However, I see the light of battle in Garrow's eye which is a comfort ...[138]

Tommy seems to have faced a choice at this point. Should he go along with the idea (first mooted a year earlier, before Lytton had fallen for Roger, and now revived) that he should effectively replace Ralph as 'the third leg of the tripod' at Ham Spray? Or should he mend fences with his family, marry Julia (with a financial settlement), and live with her at Swallowcliffe? Or might he do both?

A further clue as to Tommy's motives for marriage is hinted at in the memoirs of Kathleen 'Bobby' Hale. Three years older than Tommy, Bobby was a talented artist who became friendly with

---

* Presumably meaning that Sir Thomas had now got to hear the shocking news that Tommy had been cohabiting with Julia in Paris: Lady Tomlin had already heard it in March.

Lytton with Dadie
Rylands

Duncan and Vanessa in the early 1920s: through them she met
Tommy, was much affected by his charm, and almost certainly
had an affair with him. (She was probably included in the list of
Tommy's lovers inscribed by Bunny on Tommy's studio wall in 1923.)
She writes: 'He once said he thought he ought to marry me because
he believed I might be able to make him work.'[139] This was probably not meant seriously; but it suggests that what Tommy sought
in a wife was a muse, someone to inspire and encourage him in his
artistic labours. Certainly this was a role Julia was happy to assume.
Her main qualm was caused by his rampant promiscuity, on which
subject he wrote to reassure her: 'I used [he was twenty-six] to be
unable to stop myself making love to everyone, man, woman &
child, all the time. And now for the most part, except for periodic
outbursts, I do not do that… You perhaps imagined that my love

for you was like the feelings I have about amorous strangers…
Those feelings are perfectly momentary – arise in 10 minutes &
subside in 2 hours; this feeling I have about you has gone on for
hours, days, months, & saturates everything I do or think about.'[140]

We have two intriguing glimpses of Tommy in June 1927. At the
start of that month he was relinquishing his studio in Hampstead
and moving to Swallowcliffe, while Julia was visiting friends in
Wales. He wrote to her soon after his arrival in Wiltshire to report
his recent doings. Before leaving London he had had a 'delightful'
dinner with Bunny, an 'adorable' meeting with Duncan and
Vanessa, and an outing to the cinema with Alix. The day before
his departure, he had woken 'conscious that I had a great many
things to do, with the usual result that I did nothing but lounge'.
In the train he had encountered 'the most shattering male beauty
on his way to country house cricket'. He had arrived at the 'sweet
and peaceful' scene of the cottage to discover with alarm a mass of
parcels and packing cases. 'Mother simply ran amok at the Army
& Navy Stores. You have never seen so many slop pails, bath mats,
rugs & jugs & rolling pins … enough blankets to set up a hospital
& eiderdowns & a feather bed & some cut-glass objects like you
get for winning the sack race… I shudder to think what my mother
must have spent on it all, I only wish we could have had the money
and done it ourselves.' He concluded: 'Darling, I do miss you
so. The cottage is really very comfortable now: I'm sure you can
be happy here… So shall I write to my father & say we are going
to be married? What do you think? I don't want to be without
you & living in sin will be a complicated business… Will you write
to me, darling? I wonder if you miss me at all?'

The other account is from the pen of Frances Marshall.
Although she had not yet started keeping a regular diary, during
a weekend at Ham Spray in the second half of June Lytton suggested, as an exercise, that each of the residents write a detailed
account of their day there, and Frances kept hers (the others do not

seem to survive). The party consisted of Lytton and Carrington, Ralph and Frances, Tommy and Julia, and Alix (without James). Tommy behaved as an integral member of the household: in the drawing room he held forth with his back to the fireplace, a position normally reserved for the host. Lytton was clearly under his spell: he spent the morning talking to Tommy in the garden; after tea, he waited until Julia had left the room, whereupon he took Tommy off for a walk. (Frances remarks that, whereas Ralph, if he had been talking to Lytton, would later relate the substance of the conversation to her, it was unlikely that Tommy ever did so to Julia – he was 'too secretive'.) Ralph told Frances that 'Lytton had confessed to having put a love letter under what he believed to be Tommy's door'. (This reads oddly – is one to suppose that he got the wrong door?) We are given snatches of Tommy's conversation: he said insightful things about Virginia's new novel *To the Lighthouse*, and during lunch he had an argument with Alix (apparently they enjoyed arguing) on the subject of greed. Frances took the opportunity to question Julia, her old schoolfriend, on the state of her relations with Tommy. Julia told her that '[living together at] Swallowcliffe is definitely impossible unless Tommy and I are married – but I wouldn't be surprised if we do get married'. Frances comments: 'I don't believe that she is really in love with Tommy, but it might rescue her from what she fears may be an unhappy future, and so make her happier. If only Tommy weren't so neurotic and alarmingly destructive, but of course he's extremely intelligent, and this weekend he has been sane and charming.'[141]

Soon afterwards, Tommy and Julia did decide to marry. Julia later wrote that, although she had not been in love with him, she believed him to be a genius, and felt she might have a dignified future as the wife of a genius. Julia's father Oliver, stepmother Ray and 'Aunt Loo' were all pleased by the news, doubtless glad to be relieved of further responsibility for her. Ray (who was inspired to paint a somewhat cartoon-like picture of Tommy) wrote that

Ray Strachey's painting of Tommy

'the young man is exceedingly nice and I think it a mercy'; Alys thought Tommy 'a very nice fellow' and Julia 'a lucky girl'.[142] Julia had still to meet Tommy's parents, an encounter which proved alarming. As she wrote to Carrington:

Last night I dined with mère & père T. She was very gracious
& beaming. Not so *he*. Helen the sister ... was most genial &
gay & intelligent... I came bursting into the stately drawing
room ¼ of an hour late, & tripped up over an extraordinary
contraption in front of the fire, practically taking a header into
Lady T's swelling bosom. I poured forth hysterical apologies ...
which were listened to in courteous silence ... & we all trooped
down to the evening meal.

Fortunately Sir Thomas got on well with Oliver over luncheon
at the Oriental Club, and a financial arrangement was agreed,
assuring the couple a modest income.[143]

Some of Tommy's former lovers were upset by the news. Angus
Davidson was frankly distressed. Lincoln Kirstein, who though
just twenty had been besotted by Tommy for the past three years,*
writes in his memoirs that 'desolate envy obliged me to acknowledge [Julia's] triumph with the presentation of a single rose'.[144]
Carrington was presumably delighted that the match she had
been trying to bring about for a year had finally come to pass. As
for Lytton, his reaction may be gauged by the present he gave the
couple – a bed. ('We will think of you often on the tenderest occasions', wrote Tommy in his letter of thanks.) But Tommy continued
to be attentive to Lytton, who seems to have felt that the marriage
would amount to little more than a temporary interruption of
their relationship. As Lytton wrote on 19 July to his confidante
Mary Hutchinson:

I am leading a decidedly queer life. Both Tommy and Dadie are
devoted to me – and I to them; though to be sure, the ways are

* Writing in June 1968 to the London bookseller Heywood Hill, Kirstein declared
that he would 'gladly have died' for Tommy, whom he had 'loved more than life itself'
(information from Simon Frazer).

different!' ... My relation with Tommy is exciting – there is strength there – and a mind – a remarkable character – but there is to be a lull in the proceedings, for he is to be married on Thursday (I believe). There is also a lull with Dadie, who has gone to Cambridge – a delightful, gay affair that one. So you see altogether I have plenty to think about in my seclusion... Was there ever such a world? Such lives? Such peculiarities?[145]

The wedding (to please Tommy's parents – the couple would have preferred a civil ceremony) took place at St Pancras Church in London on 22 July 1927, and is described in a letter from Virginia Woolf to Vanessa Bell.

We went to Tommies [sic] wedding at St Pancras Church yesterday, a prosaic affair, though the service always fills my eyes with tears. Also the grotesqueness is so great. The Strachey women were of inconceivable drabness on one side, Aunt Loo having also an aroma of hypocrisy about her which makes me vomit;[†] on the other side sat the Judge in frock coat and top hat, like a shop walker. He got locked into his pew, and could not get out, except at the last moment, to sign the register. He mistook the hinge for a door handle. Julia was highly self possessed, and then Angus [Davidson] was glowering behind us. I daresay he takes it to heart, though I repeat for the 1000th time: I cannot see the physical charm of that little woodpecker man. They dined with us afterwards. I handed on your curse, just before the ceremony – Nessa's curse on marriage, it is called; and has been known to strike a Bride dead on the altar steps.[146]

Alas, the curse would be amply fulfilled.

---

* This could be interpreted as meaning that his friendship with Tommy had a physical dimension, whereas that with Dadie was essentially platonic.
† As Julia had ample caused to know, she was a pious and moralising Quaker.

Tommy and Julia

Tommy and Julia sitting in the doorway of Tommy's studio at Swallowcliffe

VI

SWALLOWCLIFFE

1927–1930

Swallowcliffe is a village in the Vale of Wardour in south-west Wiltshire, near the borders with Dorset and Hampshire, midway between Salisbury in the east and Shaftesbury in the west. It is small – the parish today has some 200 souls, and was probably not much bigger in the 1920s. The nearest sizeable town is Tisbury, three miles distant, with a population (now as probably then) of some 2,250, where the trains stop on the way from Waterloo to Exeter. It features a wood, a chalk down, and several rushing streams. Like Chaldon, the landscape is ancient, remote and mystical. Primitive jewellery found in Kent together with human skeletons estimated to be 400,000 years old has been geologically proved to come from the area. There is much evidence of iron age and bronze age activity, of burial grounds and henges and stone circles. It was a thriving community in Saxon times, most of its present paths, roads and boundaries dating from before the Norman conquest. The area flourished in the thirteenth century, its quarries providing stone for the building of Salisbury Cathedral and its sheep contributing to the wool trade, but never recovered from the Black Death in the 1350s. In the eighteenth century it was absorbed into the extensive local estates, based on Wilton, of the Herbert family, Earls of Pembroke. After the First World War, the Pembrokes, faced with death duties, sold off the parish, and a process began whereby Swallowcliffe (though for a long time it retained much of its original character) gradually ceased to be a

Mill Cottage

Breakfast at Mill Cottage

In the garden

village of farmers and craftsmen and its buildings mostly became
weekend retreats for Londoners. By the mid-1920s Swallowcliffe
Manor had thus become detatched from the farm over which it
had once presided; and the seventeenth-century Mill House, by
a swift stream about a mile from the village, had ceased to be a
working mill and been bought by Olive Powell, owner of a London
antique shop, who lived there periodically with her husband Jack.
Olive's father, Colonel Crompton, was a family friend of the
Tomlins, and through this connection Tommy learnt that the Mill
House grounds included a neglected but attractive stone cottage
which the Powells were willing to restore and let at a modest
rent.[147] He visited it in September 1926, liked it and agreed to take
it; the building work needed to make it habitable was done while
he was in Paris over the winter, and he moved there in June 1927.

This became the home of Tommy and Julia on their marriage in
July, and would remain their base for the next three years. It was

Tommy with Frances Marshall

reasonably commodious, with three rooms on the ground floor, and bedrooms above; attached to it was a byre which Tommy converted into a studio. They created a garden, engaged a young maid, Agnes, who came in daily from the village, and acquired a small white cat. Their first visitor, Carrington, who arrived on 21 September, wrote to Lytton that she found the setting enchanting, and her hosts leading an apparently idyllic life. 'Tommy was busy drawing plans of the gates of Lincoln's Inn and Julia making scones in the kitchen. The cottage looks very nice inside. Really, it's the equal to Ham Spray in elegance and comfort, only cleaner and tidier. Julia in high spirits, and both of them seemed very happy… The cooking is really very good. Julia teaches the maid herself, with Mrs Beeton sitting like an immense goddess on the kitchen table.' A couple of days later she reported that 'yesterday passed very quickly talking, cooking, drawing, walking to the post & sewing in the evening whilst Julia read Dryden to us… I thought the country very romantic on our walk to the post office. Sloping green fields & orchards & drooping thatched cottages. A slightly moth eaten & melancholy air over the village. The post office was like an Alice in Wonderland invention. I was surprised to see an old lady with spectacles and not a sheep appear. Simply a cottage kitchen, hung with china & stuffed birds in cases & artificial flowers, pitch dark with only a little table & an inkpot & a money box to prove it was a post office.' It was hilarious accompanying Julia to Tisbury to do the shopping: she had the vaguest idea of prices and quantities, though quickly made friends with the shopkeepers and market traders.[148]

In his essay on Tommy's sculpture, Oliver Garnett (Bunny's grandson) writes that 'those earliest years at Swallowcliffe were the happiest of Tommy's life'. He certainly did some impressive work there during 1927 and 1928. At the time he moved there (as mentioned by Carrington), he was busy designing a set of gates and ornamental wrought-iron railings for Lincoln's Inn, to enclose a new garden: these had been offered as a gift to the Inn by Tommy's father, one of the Inn's governors or 'benchers', possibly as a means

The Tomlin Gates at Lincoln's Inn: the initials 'T.H.' refer to the Inn's then Treasurer, Thomas Hughes

of helping Tommy. It was a difficult project, as the responsible committee rejected several drawings; but the final result, which was installed in the autumn of 1928, and stands to this day, was of great elegance.[149] In the spring of 1928 he carved an elaborate granite bench for an Oxford college, which necessitated a visit to the granite quarries in Cornwall (where he and Julia stayed at the Tinner's Arms, Zennor, his destination during his 'flight' from Oxford in 1919). Also in 1928 he completed three fine portrait heads – of his wife Julia, his sister Helen, and Igor, the fourteen-year-old son of Boris Anrep. That same year he designed a relief for the exterior of Ham Spray, though this ended in disaster when the plaster structure fell off the wall, and smashed. As Oliver Garnett writes: 'The disasters which constantly befell Tommy's sculpture became the subject of sympathetic amusement among his friends.' Tommy himself does not seem to have minded unduly. As he wrote to Bunny in 1927: 'I take the greatest pleasure in working all day at things which I know I am going to smash up when they are finished; all the pleasure of doing it, and none of that extraneous and vain anxiety about its success, whether it will please my friends or some unlucky gull who has commissioned it.'[150]

Ham Spray – some forty miles from Swallowcliffe, in the north-east corner of the county – continued to be a second home for both Tommy and Julia. They stayed there together at Christmas 1927, Easter 1928 and Christmas 1928. Tommy also went there on his own, to keep Lytton company. Julia was an ideal wife in that she never objected to Tommy going alone to stay with the men who loved him: indeed, Carrington, on her first visit to Swallow-cliffe, wrote to Lytton that Julia 'very much resents the idea that T. can't be asked away without her … so just you take that to heart & ask T. whenever you want him alone'. However, when she wrote these words, Tommy's standing with Lytton was about to undergo a slight but significant shift. On 13 September, Philip Ritchie, who had been Lytton's great love a couple of years earlier, suddenly

Tommy's bust of Julia

died of pneumonia following the removal of his tonsils, aged twenty-eight. Roger Senhouse, his friend whom he had introduced to Lytton, was devastated; their shared loss had the effect of bringing about a reconciliation between Roger and Lytton, who had been estranged for the previous six months. Thus the (unattached) Roger was restored to his former position as Lytton's overriding romantic interest, and the lingering notion (which Tommy's marriage to Julia had not quite dispelled) that Tommy might eventually live at Ham Spray as Lytton's helpmeet was quietly dropped.

Nevertheless, Lytton remained deeply fond of Tommy, whom he helped (for Tommy was perpetually short of money) with a stream of commissions. Apart from the ill-fated relief mentioned above, these included a set of cupid-like figures for the Ham Spray interior, and a statuette representing the scene in Rabelais where

Tommy and Julia at
Ham Spray

Pantagruel wipes his posterior with the neck of a goose. (This
was originally intended as the model for a fountain statue, which
for some reason was never made.)[151] Then, at the end of 1928, soon
after *Elizabeth and Essex* had been published and become a run-
away success on both sides of the Atlantic, Lytton commissioned
Tommy, on generous terms, to do a bust of himself. The sittings
took place at Ham Spray in August 1929. 'I sit all day to Tommy',
wrote Lytton to Dadie, 'who is creating what appears to me a
highly impressive, repulsive and sinister object.'[152] However, when
he finally received the bronze cast in November, he was delighted.
'Most impressive', he wrote to Tommy, 'almost menacingly so, and

altogether, so far as I can judge, very successful.' He was determined that it should be exhibited: he gave a party in Bloomsbury
to show it off to his friends, and had another cast made for public
display at the Leicester Galleries. Bunny thought it 'the most
distinguished and accomplished head you have ever done', and
ordered a lead cast for himself. Meanwhile the bronze cast on display was bought by a young collector named Brinsley Ford, who
subsequently presented it to the Tate Gallery – the first of Tommy's
works to enter a public collection.[153] Tommy's masterstroke (in
the view of Oliver Garnett) was to present Lytton's beard and
spectacles as a kind of disguise behind which he peers out – with
amused intelligence, and a touch of weary cynicism – at the world.

By the time Tommy sculpted Lytton a new element had entered
the Ham Spray constellation, as Carrington – who felt lonely after
Lytton's reconciliation with Roger, and had finally terminated her
long and unsatisfactory relationship with Gerald Brenan – was in
the midst of an affair with Bernard 'Beakus' Penrose, youngest (born
1904) of the four Penrose brothers (whose interests, unlike those
of his siblings, were sporting rather than artistic or intellectual – by
his mid-twenties he had become a noted yachtsman). This would
end in tragedy: at the end of 1929, Carrington discovered she was
pregnant by Beakus; not wishing to have a child, she had Ralph
(who continued to feel responsible for her as a husband) arrange an
abortion; and Frances, who longed to have a child by Ralph, was so
upset by the situation that she (already depressed for other reasons)
suffered something of a breakdown.[154] However, while the affair
was proceeding, Beakus, an enthusiastic amateur film-maker, produced several home movies at Ham Spray, one of which, just three
minutes long, features Tommy and Julia.* Two men and two women
emerge from a country house in Edwardian attire. The younger
man, a floppy-haired bohemian (Tommy), sets up an easel and

---

* It may be seen on YouTube at https://www.youtube.com/watch?v= FFOOG9PjlJc
(starting seven and a half minutes into the clip).

Above: Tommy adding the final touches to Lytton's bust at Ham Spray, 1929: on the right is a glimpse of Carrington's painting of Tidmarsh Mill, the former home of herself and Lytton, on the left a glimpse of Tommy's bust of Henrietta, which he had presented to Carrington

Left: The finished masterpiece

starts to paint; the younger woman (Julia) gives him an affectionate kiss, then goes off for a stroll with the other two (Julia's father Oliver, and Carrington). Eventually the artist gets bored, throws aside his canvas and wanders about, until he discovers a seated young lady with a parasol (a dummy). His eyes light up with demonic lust and he sets about seducing her, but is discovered by the three strollers, who attack him with their umbrellas and walking sticks while he defends himself with the parasol – a scene executed in 'knockabout' style. At twenty-eight, Tommy's features are handsome but haggard, and he displays both animal magnetism and some acting ability; from what one knows of his life, the theme is distinctly near the bone. Though this was no masterpiece, it inspired Tommy to think of making another, longer film for commercial release, in which he would play a baronet-cum-white-slave-trafficker – 'seeing him act the rake in the Ham Spray film I believe he would do it splendidly', wrote Julia to Carrington.[155] Nothing came of the project.

At Swallowcliffe, Tommy and Julia had frequent weekend visitors. Apart from Carrington (Lytton was too much of a sybarite to stay with them), these included Tommy's brother Garrow; Bunny Garnett; Alix Strachey (usually without James, who had been rather upset by Julia's marrying Tommy); Frances and Ralph; Barbara Bagenal; Eddy Sackville-West (who remained under the spell of Tommy, and sometimes had him and Julia to stay at Knole); John Banting; Roy Harrod; and Julia's friend Hester Chapman (now married to the owner of a preparatory school in Wales). Sometimes they gave weekend parties, such as one thrown to celebrate Tommy's twenty-seventh birthday in March 1928: as the cottage could only accommodate two or three guests, the others stayed at the village pub. Sometimes, when money was tight, they took in paying guests – it was on this basis that, in the summer of 1928, they accommodated Julia's half-sister Barbara Strachey, aged sixteen, whose parents wanted her off their hands for a few weeks.

It was an uncomfortable episode, as Eddy was also staying: he could not abide her, while Barbara (as Julia discovered by surreptitiously reading her diary) had conceived an unlikely crush on him. (For that matter, Julia did not care for Eddy, whom she found 'acid & dry as ashes … next year his shoulder bones will have grown clean through his thin grey flannel suit & his teeth will show through his cheeks & he … will finally have to be stuffed & put in a glass case'.) A new friend of Tommy who stayed in January 1929 was Cyril Connolly, just becoming famous as a journalist, who since coming down from Oxford in 1925 had been a protégé of Julia's rich step-great-uncle Logan Pearsall Smith. After a fierce intellectual discussion touching upon homosexuality, the nature of freedom, and the relative merits of classicism and romanticism, Connolly concluded that Tommy was 'altogether the most interesting young person I have met, and I felt I hadn't seen nearly enough of him'[156] – high praise coming from such a source.

A regular visitor who held a special place in Tommy's affections was his sister Helen. After graduating from Oxford in 1928, where she had read Modern Languages at Somerville, she was expected by her parents to become a companion to her mother at Clifton Place, while looking around for a suitable matrimonial prospect; but Helen was determined to avoid this stultifying fate and to continue her academic career, enrolling for a one-year Diploma in Anthropology at London University. Tommy, who worked on her portrait head around this time, staunchly supported her in her chosen path, writing an amusing poem (reproduced as Appendix II) satirising the life their parents seemed to envisage for her. Having received her diploma, Helen landed a job as curator of the Pitt-Rivers Ethnographical Museum at Farnham in Dorset, just a dozen miles from Swallowcliffe, enabling her to see much more of Tommy.

Apart from the Powells at the Mill House, the Tomlins knew various people who lived within a fifteen-mile radius of Swallowcliffe (though as they never owned a car, in order to visit them they had either to walk heroic distances or rely on lifts, public transport or taxi services). These included the local culture-vulture, Miss Edith Olivier (1872–1948). Edith was the daughter of the Vicar of Wilton, the great property near Salisbury of the Earls of Pembroke. She had studied at Oxford, and been decorated after the First World War for her role in the Women's Land Army. After her father's death in 1919 the Pembrokes put the former estate dairy, converted into a comfortable villa with a garden, at her disposal, where she founded a *salon* of artists and writers (she herself was an aspiring novelist). She had a distinct preference for young homosexual men, such as Lord Pembroke's younger brother David Herbert, and the rising artist Rex Whistler. Even before Tommy had gone to live at Swallowcliffe Edith had heard he was coming* and was determined to include him in her circle. When he moved to the cottage in June 1927, she persuaded him to visit her. He reported to Julia that he found her 'rather horrid. Very vivacious and up to date, elderly, withered, smartish, with dyed hair & curious greenish eyebrows, and not very bright in the head. However she made herself as pleasant as she could in the oil & vinegar style.' Edith meanwhile wrote of Tommy in her diary: 'He has a fine imaginative face. Rather short. But not bad figure. Very easy to talk to.'[157] Several of her protégés turned up, notably Stephen Tennant, aged twenty-one, who lived nearby at Wilsford Manor: a gifted dilettante, neurotic and frail, he was a much handsomer version of Eddy Sackville-West. 'The conversation [wrote Tommy to Julia] was entirely about the Blackbirds [a singing group], & the gramophone played incessantly. Stephen T. said, "Too deliciously savage, don't you think?"' Tommy (though he admitted to fancying Tennant) was glad to get away.

---

* From her friend Dorothy Tomlin, Tommy's aunt, whose husband, the Revd James ('Jimmy') Tomlin (1871–1959), the judge's younger brother, was a leading Wiltshire cleric, being Principal of the Missionary College at Warminster and Prebendary of Salisbury Cathedral.

Edith got into the habit of dropping in to the Tomlins' cottage whenever she happened to be passing. She adored Tommy, but did not at first care for Julia. Calling on them soon after their arrival, she wrote that he was 'so nice, radiant & alive' while she seemed 'a cross, dead, wooden thing without beauty – strange that he loves her so'. They came to dread both her unannounced visits and her frequent invitations. The first time Julia accompanied Tommy to visit Edith at Wilton, they felt so uncomfortable that they left early, and had to wait two hours for their bus. However, for all her absurdity Edith was quite perceptive. She came to see that Julia, though withdrawn, was intelligent ('she says little, but what she says is *real*'), and noticed that she encouraged him to shine in company. Eventually they accepted an invitation to spend a weekend with her, to study the sculpture at Wilton House – though Tommy teased her by expressing aggressively atheist and socialist views (which he did not really hold) to the staunchly Anglican and Tory Edith throughout the visit.[158] The years 1927–30 marked the heyday of the hedonistic, party-going set known as 'the bright young people', and Edith, though getting on for sixty, was adopted by them as an honorary member – she was friendly with several of their leading lights, and enjoyed their frivolous antics. Though Tommy and Julia had several friends who were involved in this world (such as Julia's old flame Eddie Gathorne-Hardy), it was not one in which either of them felt comfortable. In April 1930 Cecil Beaton, the fashionable photographer, then twenty-six, mentioned to Edith that he longed to have a Wiltshire cottage for weekend parties. She told him that she had recently heard from Tommy that he had discovered on his rambles a hidden gem of a run-down Georgian manor, used as a farm building. Despite the fact that Edith, as a lark, had done herself up that afternoon as 'a Matisse portrait', with extravagant garments and a grotesquely painted face, she, Rex Whistler, David Herbert, and the two Paget sisters (bright young females) piled with Beaton into his car and they all drove off to call on Tommy, who, clad in his sculptor's overalls, guided them to Ashcombe, the house in question.[159] Although Beaton promptly rented it from the farmer who owned it, and was soon giving parties there which became famous for dressing-up and every sort of high jinks, there is no evidence that Tommy attended these – if invited, he did not care to go.

A household more to Tommy's taste was that of Augustus John (1878–1961), who early in 1927 moved with his wife Dorelia and their children to Fryern Court on the edge of the New Forest, an large property about half an hour's drive from Swallowcliffe where they kept open house for their enormous acquaintance. Augustus had a number of links to Tommy: he was a friend and patron of Frank Dobson; Tommy's sometime lover Bobby Hale had been his secretary in the early 1920s; and his wife and daughters were close to Carrington. Though separated by almost a quarter of a century in age, Augustus and Tommy had three things in common which drew them together: a manic-depressive nature, a fondness for drink, and unbridled promiscuity (though John confined his interest to women – when asked if he had ever considered

Tommy with Carrington at Fryern Court

the alternative, he replied that there were 'not enough hours in the day'). Life at Fryern was so informal and alcoholic that few records exist tracing the endless comings and goings; but we know that Tommy and Julia accompanied Carrington to a party there to see in the new year of 1928 which was so wild that some of the guests found themselves unable to leave for several days. In his memoirs, Augustus mentions that Tommy, who 'was always ready to make a journey in any direction with anybody at any moment', was his companion when he went to Wales in 1931 to deliver the address at the gipsy funeral of his friend John Sampson.[160] Another artist closely associated with Augustus, who became a friend of Tommy, was Henry Lamb (1883-1960). Lytton, of whom he painted a famous portrait, had once been unrequitedly in love with Henry, who was a frequent guest at Ham Spray. After Henry's marriage in the summer of 1928 to Lady Pansy Pakenham, they moved to Coombe Bissett in Dorset, a village within each reach of Swallow-cliffe. When they visited Mill Cottage soon afterwards, Tommy and Julia (as the latter wrote to Frances) 'enjoyed their company very much *indeed* … Pansy's sophisticated manner, gurgling voice

Julia drawn by Henry Lamb

and dazzling beauty are quite a treat, don't you agree?'[161] Henry was to paint portraits of both Julia and Tommy.

Two families who lived not far from Swallowcliffe were rich, and showed much generosity to Tommy and Julia. Sir Ernest Debenham owned the department store of that name, which he sold in 1927 to devote himself to dairy farming (and the creation of a model village for his estate workers) at Bladen, Dorset. The Tomlins got to know the Debenhams as one of the many children of the latter, Audrey, was a friend of Tommy's sister Helen. When Julia fell ill, they made their London house in Addison Road available for her recuperation.[162] Hugo Pitman (1892–1963) – stockbroker, sportsman, war hero, art collector and friend of royalty (and *alumnus* of New College, Oxford) – was married to Reine, niece of the artist John Singer Sargent, and built himself a house at Odstock near Salisbury. Hugo and Reine once invited Tommy and Julia to join them for 'a week in Paris at their expense in a hotel', which seems to have been enjoyed by all. (If one is to believe Julia's letter to Carrington, something of a wife-swap took place, as she writes that 'Tommy … had a go at the adorable Reine', while she herself 'fell madly in love with the Scotchman [Hugo]'.) Another taste of high-life occurred when Tommy's cousin and godfather Orme Clarke (1880–1949), the heir to the family baronetcy,* who had married a Roosevelt heiress, invited them to spend Easter 1929 at Bibury Court, their country house in Gloucestershire – in honour of which occasion the Tomlins, who rarely spent much money on clothes, splashed out on some expensive tailoring. As Julia related breathlessly to Carrington:

> Mrs Clarke has inherited the Roosevelt millions I gather, & everything is very much up to snuff… Each bedroom has its bathroom, & marble bath appointments & so forth. There are

---

* As a colonial civil servant he had distinguished himself by creating the legal system of British Palestine. He succeeded his great-uncle the General as the 4th Clarke baronet in 1932.

hard courts, squash racket courts, a private steeple chase course, hunters & racers by the dozen. At meals one footman's sole employment was to perpetually bring round 3 different kinds of bread on a tray … making it quite impossible to have any cohesion in conversation with one's neighbours … Mrs Clark is … the Darkest Horse I've ever met in my life … her manner strange beyond dreams … The steeplechasing boys were also very rum. Orme himself—They were extraordinarily nice to us, an amiable family – but how unearthly! Perhaps all rich people are.

London was an easy rail journey from Tisbury, and Tommy and Julia often went there either singly or together. Tommy continued to attend the monthly dinners of the Cranium Club, and had business in the capital, notably with the founders who cast his sculptures, Fiorini of Chelsea. (Tommy also used the sexual services of a beautiful youth belonging to this Italian family of craftsmen, an indulgence which proved costly. 'Do you think Lytton could lend me a little money?', wrote Tommy to Carrington. '"The Little Flower" [a literal English rendering of "Fiorini"] is proving rather a drain!'[163]) They kept in touch with their Bloomsbury friends, and attended their parties: in November 1929, Julia describes a London visit during which they enjoyed one dinner with Virginia, Leonard, Vanessa and Duncan, another with Ralph, Frances and Clive, a third with Lytton (featuring the eccentric ceramics expert Billy Winkworth), and a fourth with the Hugo Pitmans following which they went to the Blue Lantern nightclub with the outrageously drunk Eddie Gathorne-Hardy. There were many friends with whom they were normally able to stay, though once, when Tommy was summoned at short notice to discuss the Lincoln's Inn gates, they found themselves lodging with

Tommy's old landlady's up at Golders Green (on account of her cheapness). My dear, a *single* bed only, for both of us, no bath, no soap, & ¼ hour's walk from nearest underground, & this for four or five nights. Tommy loved it, so don't mention I said it was uncomfortable, he loves his old landlady bless her heart. She is a dear soul it is true, Italian or something, & wore a brocade bandeau & orange woollen carpet slippers with the heels worn quite away. She brought us warm water to wash with in the mornings in the palms of her hands, I believe, for there was never any sign of a jug when she had vanished away, & when we came to wash it was icy cold of course.

As will be seen, in 1930 Tommy started renting a studio at 8, Percy Street, Fitzrovia, which served for a time as their London base.

Following his marriage, Tommy's relations with his parents seem to have been reasonably good. His mother sometimes stayed with them at Swallowcliffe. 'We whirled all over Wiltshire with Lady T.', wrote Julia to Carrington in June 1929, '& very much enjoyed ourselves to our intense surprise.' Every year the judge rented a large country house for six weeks of August and September, and Tommy and Julia looked forward to joining the family party there, to which they were usually able to invite some of their friends. In 1928, the 'summer villa' was Smedmore in Dorset, a romantic William and Mary house on the coast not far from Chaldon Herring, the ancestral seat of the Mansel family. 'What a life here!', wrote Julia. 'Evening dress, and a bedroom as large as a ballroom with private bath.' In 1929, the house was Angley Park near Cranbrook in Kent, owned by distant Tomlin cousins. 'We are not having a bad time by any means', wrote Julia. '36 mouths to feed at every meal, the old cook says. A lake, a park, fascinating red-haired goddesses, strange dark elfin beings ... It is charmingly pretty, in the style of 1830.' In 1930 Tommy's widowed Aunt Bessie died and her brother the judge inherited Upper Hardres Manor, the scene of Tommy's childhood holidays, which henceforth hosted the annual family reunion: building works were undertaken to refurbish the old house, for which Tommy was commissioned to design some pillars and

The recently ennobled Lord Tomlin with two of his grandchildren at Angley Park, 1929

mouldings. Tommy's nephew Philip Trower, born in 1924, retained happy recollections (in 2017) of how he and his siblings loved being with Tommy during these summer visits. 'Children seemed to bring out what was best in him. He was always full of fun, introducing us to new games, telling us amusing stories about people and things.'[164] Meanwhile the family had experienced an enhancement in its social status. In February 1929, Sir Thomas Tomlin was promoted to the highest rank of the judiciary when he was appointed a Lord of Appeal in Ordinary, or 'law lord', with a peerage. It was a rare case of a High Court judge being translated to the House of Lords – the highest court in the land – without passing through the intermediate stage as a judge of the Court of Appeal. Julia was amused to learn that, as the daughter-in-law of a peer, she would henceforth be formally known as 'the Honourable Mrs Stephen Tomlin'.

To outward appearances, the marriage of Tommy and Julia was happy, and they led a fulfilling life together. Certainly this was the impression they generally gave when they received visitors, or visited other people. But all was not what it seemed. Four factors bedeviled their married life from the very beginning.

The first was lack of money. At first sight, this seems odd. On the one hand, they had a private income (mostly from Tomlin family sources) which ought to have been adequate for their needs,* in addition to what Tommy managed to earn from his sculpture. On the other hand, they had few obvious regular outgoings apart from the expense of running their cottage; and they lived quite frugally. They did not own a car. They spent little money on clothes. They did not take holidays, except to stay with friends. They rarely travelled abroad.† They had rich and generous friends who often picked up the bills. Yet Julia's letters to Carrington mention almost constant financial difficulties. After a year of marriage, she wrote that they were seriously overdrawn and needed to economise rigorously during the coming months. At times they were obliged to take in paying guests, or stay with friends while they let the cottage. In 1929 Tommy announced that, as an economy measure, they would be neither giving nor receiving Christmas presents that year. Three possible explanations suggest themselves (all of which no doubt played a role): that they were inept at managing their affairs; that they had expenses which were not apparent to the casual observer; and that the normal, modest tenor of their existence was punctuated by episodes of improvidence (certainly

---

*   When the couple separated in 1934, Tommy's father announced that he was reducing the annual sum he allowed Tommy to £300 – so the allowance had presumably amounted to considerably more during the marriage. Julia also continued to receive an allowance from her stepmother's family.

†   The correspondence suggests that, during the first two and a half years of their marriage, they went abroad together only once – to Portofino, probably in 1929. It was on the return journey that they enjoyed the week in Paris with the Pitmans (mentioned above) at the latter's expense.

Tommy aspired to be a generous host when he played the role, and was known to give expensive presents).

The second factor was Tommy's drinking, which seems to have got out of hand quite early in the marriage. As they lived in a fairly heavy-drinking world, in which getting tipsy at parties, or going to bed in a stupor, were commonplace, this was not immediately apparent to their friends (several of whom, notably Augustus John, rivalled Tommy in their alcoholic consumption); but at some point Tommy crossed a line and began a descent into serious dipsomania. On a visit to Chaldon Herring in 1930 he called on Valentine Ackland, the new young friend of Sylvia Townsend Warner who had bought her a cottage in the village (though they had not yet started living together). Knowing of Tommy's rejection of Sylvia, Valentine, who was herself a secret alcoholic, was at first hostile to him; but her feelings soon turned to pity, 'for he was going down my path, I could see. He was already half destroyed by drink.'[165] The effects of alcohol were compounded in Tommy's case by the fact that he was also a user of narcotic drugs. For obvious reasons, there is scant reference to this in the contemporary sources. But Julia, in her account of their marriage which she wrote following its final breakdown in 1934,[166] mentions various aspects of his appearance and behaviour – his extreme pallor and lack of facial expression; his 'strangely fixed unfocused eyes'; his tendency to spend long periods in a trance, and weep for no apparent reason; and a self-absorption which left little room for affectionate or concerned feelings towards her or anyone else – which are characteristic of the abuse of 'hard' drugs, especially opiates.

The third problem was that, whereas Julia did not particularly enjoy sex, Tommy had a powerful libido which required constant gratification. (Indeed, although they shared a bed, there is some evidence that their marriage was only intermittently consummated, and eventually became largely platonic in character.) Consequently, Tommy took his pleasure where he found it with whomever of either sex he managed to get his hands on – at Swallowcliffe, in London, or wherever he happened to be.* Julia turned a blind eye to these escapades, and indeed may have felt a certain relief when he found an outlet for his urges. Nevertheless, it must have been humiliating for her that Tommy generally found sexual pleasure with almost anyone but her; and what she *did* crave was his affection – which was certainly present at the outset of their marriage, but became less evident with the passing years. One habit of Tommy's which tested her tolerance was that, on visits to London, he sometimes arranged for working-class young people of either sex to visit Swallowcliffe, ostensibly to model for his sculpture – who would join them at mealtimes, and towards whom Julia was expected to play the gracious hostess. In November 1928 (as she wrote to Carrington) one such female invitee descended on them for a fortnight, Tommy paying her £4 a week for her services – though Tommy soon admitted that he found the inanity of her conversation maddening, and even Julia drew the line when he suggested he might go to Ham Spray for the weekend, leaving the two women together. In June 1930 she mentions a visit from a male model described by the initials 'C.T.'. This is presumably the youth concerning whom an anecdote circulated among their friends which Cyril Connolly repeats in his journal:

> 'You can't do this here – not with your wife in the room,' said young man to Tommy who was assaulting him. Tommy looked at him insanely – 'Cockteaser!' – and continued.[167]

Julia writing to Carrington relates that C.T. 'when asked next morning how he had enjoyed it, said with a sweet smile that he was really rather indifferent either way'.

---

* Bunny wrote to Mina in December 1928 that 'Tommy as you know has married Julia Strachey & lives in rustic bliss, occasionally visiting town for a debauch. I was very cross with him at the last of these & abused him violently, so I suppose my love for him is as warm as ever.' (Berg Collection.)

Finally, there were the terrible depressions to which Tommy was prone (and which cannot have been helped, either in their frequency or intensity, by the drink and drugs). Whenever other people were present, he seems to have been able to put on a show of liveliness and charm; but when he and Julia were alone together, he was apt to descend into brooding, silent moods which sometimes lasted for days or even weeks – and were generally followed by torrents of remorse. While Julia usually remained loyally silent about these episodes, which she came to dread, there are muted mentions of them in her letters to Carrington. 'T's voice has lost all tone [she wrote early in 1928], his face is ever turned away when one speaks or asks a question, he retires gently but firmly from any attempt at embrace, he looks grim as death if one ventures on a playful jest ... & altogether the temperature is at once below freezing & above boiling & the weather is set stormy down in Wiltshire at present. One of these days it will suddenly veer round & skies will pour forth rays of blue again; the storm will be forgotten as a dream, & no one will be a whit wiser about the whole affair ...' In May 1929 she wrote: 'Tommy will not do any sculpting. What is rather awful is that sooner or later there will be a fearful storm of remorse & bitter repentance. "Why have I wasted all these months? I am the scum of the earth, a parasite on the face of society, life is not worth living, I wish I were dead." And when will it begin? He hasn't touched his clay since Easter; though I have tried various ruses to get him to begin working ... he won't say a word to me on the subject, just "NO!", & goes away with a set jaw & gardens & reads a book.'

In her memoir of her marriage to Tommy, Julia describes a ghastly scenario which would replay itself again and again. For days on end he would address no word to her, pay her no attention; he would stare motionless into space, sometimes groan or weep, pace the garden, go in and out of his studio, pick up a book and start reading and put it down. 'And at odd times of the day or night, without looking at me or addressing me personally, he would stare ahead into the empty air and articulate his interminable tirades, endlessly inveighing against all the Ancient Curses, Sins and Primal Glooms of the universe.' He seemed (and, she came to believe, *was*) in thrall to dark forces. Then the telephone would ring with an invitation from one of their many friends in the neighbourhood 'to join them for drinks, dinner, luncheon or a picnic expedition. And these invitations, though received by Tommy with direst groans, were nevertheless invariably accepted.' Julia continues with an astonishing description of what (as she perceived it) regularly ensued.

Once established in deck-chairs on the lawn, overlooking the sumptuous garden and drinking cocktails, Tommy would lose no time in going into action. He would set to, compelled as I could see by ... that dark spectral Demon King who was ever at his side, and collect all the scalps ... to lay at the feet of his abhorred master. Beneath the whip, he would exert himself to extract from the assembled company the heavy ritual of ... homage that was necessary to maintain the rule of his archaic Magician King. I had become familiar with ... those mighty black wings beating upon Tommy ... but invisible to the rest of the company.

The guests sitting relaxed in deck-chairs, toasting each other in the summer sunlight, seemed not to perceive the shocking pallor and mortal sickness on the sculptor's face. He afterwards confessed that what caused him most regret was the fact that, feeling cursed and guilty himself, he determined that the rest of the world should feel the same about themselves, and the happier, the more innocent the person to whom he was talking, the more vitriolic was his ambition to infect them with his sense of doom. To this end, in his famous polemical displays, he was adept at producing statements disguised as

Tommy and Julia off
to a garden party

objective truths, which were in fact heavily loaded with bitter-
ness and destructive intent. And certainly no one possessed
greater adroitness at running his illegal contraband through the
conversational customs, so to speak.

One thing was paramount. Tommy's daemon insisted that
not only with their souls but definitely with their *bodies* everyone must him worship. This was the symbol and pledge of
allegiance and subjection.

Tommy in the nude, photographed by Julia

And lo and behold, by the end of any party, everybody present – man, woman and child – had fallen in love with him. He had managed to hook the lot! Without having personally witnessed this no one could have believed it possible. But under the lash Tommy worked hard; those persons who hadn't been well and truly 'laid' by him on previous occasions, and had their scalps collected, must be laid *now* at this party. Naturally these amorous guerilla attacks took place out of sight – though only just. Maybe round a twisted corner of the terrace. Maybe indoors, up in the bathroom for instance. Those for whom there was positively no time ... were simply stored away senseless, in the game-bag, already partially de-feathered, trussed up, and almost oven-ready for some future occasion.

When the party was finally over Tommy and I would return along the Wiltshire lanes to our cottage, and only next morning did we have to face the most ruinous part of it all. All through the following day: recantation; contrition; repentance... This was the worst part of our life together, for me. If only ... Tommy could have been content with the actual sins he had committed. If only he could have done without this aftermath of tortured guilt! Then there would have been a little time left over for companionship with me ...[168]

This sounds incredible; but much of it is confirmed from other sources. Valentine Ackland wrote that, at the time of her solitary encounter with Tommy (1930), 'everyone I had recently met had been in love with him ... [and] seen him as beautiful and rare and entrancing'. (Valentine herself, knowing of his treatment of Sylvia, was resistant to his charms.) As for the 'amorous guerilla attacks', here is Alix Strachey (a professional psychologist, and also resistant) writing to Eddy Sackville-West about Tommy's behaviour at a nautical fancy-dress party given by Beakus Penrose in the flat of Ralph and Frances in Gordon Square in October 1928:

We were all dressed as sailors or boats or mermaids or seaweed ... And Julia wasn't there, but Tommy was, deadly drunk, & he tried to possess the whole of the room at once & almost burst himself. His eyes glared like a madman's, & he threw himself on man & woman alike. He ended up, I gather, by more or less raping Angus [Davidson] in public, but I wasn't there. Really, I cannot understand his sexual attraction ... There is so much scorn for the other & contempt for himself & public showing off and sadism and crudeness that the stomach rises at it ...[169]

Possibly Tommy's 'rape' of Angus was intended as a contribution to the 'nautical' flavour of the evening. Certainly when it came to sexual relations with men, buggery was his preferred *modus operandi*, judging by the following extraordinary passage in a letter from Carrington to Julia of April 1928:

> Seb[astian Sprott] & [Roger] Sen[house] were here [at Ham Spray] ... Seb in low spirits as he had been frolicking with his Ernie P.A. [*pénétration anale*] & in consequence had to have a sentinel p[ile] removed & has been forced to take liquid p. & air cushions. I told Tommy what his great creed 'of P.A. & nothing but P.A.' had led poor Seb into. But he merely rubbed his hands at getting another convert.[170]

Perhaps Tommy's 'creed of P.A.' applied to his relations with women as well as men – though he is rumoured to have fathered at least one child by his many female partners (a married woman, who passed it off as her husband's).

Early in 1930, Tommy, meeting Vanessa Bell at a party, told her that he felt rather hurt that she had never been to see them at Swallowcliffe. Consequently she stayed with them for a weekend in February. She enjoyed her visit, and like other guests had the impression that Tommy and Julia were perfectly happy together; but he admitted to her that he was 'depressed about his work'. Vanessa (who evidently knew little about the more problematic aspects of Tommy's existence) suggested that, for the sake of his career, he should leave the country and return to live in London. As she wrote to Duncan: 'He does very little in the country & seemed wanting in vitality... I am sure young artists need to rub up against each other ... & he sees no one the least interested in his work.'[171] Julia was alarmed; as she wrote to Carrington, a move to London, even if it helped Tommy's career, risked enveloping them in 'financial ruin & also the ruin of peace of mind & health. As we cannot manage to keep within our income here, what would it be like in London? & then Tommy would stay up late every night & all the old troubles would be sure to start again.' Tommy, however, took Vanessa's suggestion to heart, saying as she departed: 'If you hear of anyone wanting to rent a country cottage with a studio, let me know...'[172]

Although it would be another couple of years before they finally gave up the cottage, this episode marked the beginning of the end of their life at Swallowcliffe. Soon afterwards, Tommy started renting a studio in Percy Street off Tottenham Court Road, where he spent more and more of his time. They were still periodically together at Swallowcliffe, but more often than not the cottage was sublet to friends – when Edith Olivier next called there uninvited, she discovered it inhabited by a homosexual ménage consisting of Eddie Gathorne-Hardy, John Banting and the aesthete Brian Howard.[173] Meanwhile, in the spring of 1930, Julia departed on her own for an extended holiday with her aunt and uncle Dorothy and Simon Bussy (Oliver's sister and brother-in-law, both artists) at their farmhouse at Roquebrune on the *Côte d'Azur*. She felt that a period of separation from Tommy, whose behaviour had been particularly nightmarish of late, might help save their marriage; and she wanted to start work on a short story or novel which had been forming in her mind. On 20 May she wrote him from Roquebrune a touching letter, which suggested that, as far as the marriage was concerned, all was not yet lost.

Darling Piggy,

Write and tell me you are glad I am coming back to you soon
now; and that you are feeling happy – a little bit – about it. I
miss you, dearest, very much, and have often longed to hug you.
I am truly longing to start a joint life with you again, and am
very keen to design you some tombstones,* statues, even iron
gates if required. And will you do another head of me please,
Piggy, and help me with my story? I was unutterably miserable
when I read that you couldn't face Swallowcliffe again. Surely,
later on, we could go there – we can have very happy times
there again. But what I want to express in this letter is that I
really do love you. That I will never leave you unless you want
me to, and that I believe we can help each other to be happy
now. Even though we have been through a miserable period we
shall be so very snug together again.[174]

* Three months earlier, while they were staying with Bunny at Hilton, Tommy had
been commissioned by neighbours of the Garnetts to design a tombstone for their
stillborn child (Julia to Carrington, 23 February 1930, Berg Collection).

Tommy painted by John Strachey in 1930, when Virginia Woolf
described him as 'grown round as a snowball'

BREAKDOWN

1930–1932

During the second half of 1930 Tommy and Julia gradually transferred their base from Wiltshire to London. They rented a succession of furnished flats, few of which proved satisfactory: one problem was that they no longer shared a bed, so had the extra expense of a two-bedroom flat. The attempt to relaunch their marriage after Julia's return from her French holiday had limited success: by the end of the summer they were both in a state of gloom, their financial problems had become acute, and their domestic strains could no longer be concealed from friends. 'I wish something could be done about Tommy', wrote Lytton to Carrington on 20 September. 'Was anything said about the china figures? One commission there at any rate.' 'I expect Julia & Tommy will recover', replied Carrington, 'it's partly the end of summer that is depressing them, & their perpetual confusion over finance. I begged Tommy to get on with the china figures & he said he would.'[175] Tommy declined an invitation from Julian Bell to address the Heretics, a Cambridge intellectual club, on the grounds that 'such notions as I have in my head are of the kind that darkens the atmosphere'.[176] Though still only in his thirtieth year, he was losing his physical shape thanks to his drinking: meeting him at Saxon Sydney-Turner's fiftieth birthday party that autumn, Virginia Woolf found him 'grown round as a snowball, in the last lap of destitution'.[177] Yet there were still moments of optimism: in October we find Tommy and Julia living together at Swallowcliffe, apparently happily as of yore. Carrington stayed with them, and enjoyed herself; no doubt hoping they would continue to use Mill Cottage as their matrimonial retreat, she painted a mural over their sitting room door of 'a goddess lying by the water's brim'.[178] But their visits to the cottage (usually let to friends) became increasingly rare (though they did not relinquish the lease until mid-1932).

One factor which enriched their lives and helped shore up their

Rosamond
Lehmann and
Wogan Philipps

marriage was the friendship of two other attractive young couples who had recently become regular visitors to Ham Spray: Wogan Philipps and Rosamond Lehmann (who had married in 1928); and Bryan Guinness and Diana Mitford (who had married in 1929). Wogan and Bryan came from wealthy families (though Wogan would eventually be disinherited by his father, Lord Milford), and had been educated at Eton and Oxford; they were both handsome

Diana Mitford
and Bryan
Guinness

and charming, but rather lazy and feckless. Wogan aspired to be an artist and Bryan fancied himself a writer and poet, but neither had much talent for their respective vocations. Of far greater interest were their wives: Rosamond (who was the same age as Tommy and Julia) and Diana (who was almost a decade younger, having married Bryan when she was only eighteen) were great beauties, as well as being intelligent and gifted. Having read English at Cambridge, Rosamond, only twenty-six, had had a phenomenal success in 1927 with her novel *Dusty Answer* (a success she would never quite repeat during the remaining half-century of her writing career). Diana, third of the six soon-to-be-famous Mitford sisters, daughters of Lord Redesdale, had never received any formal education, but was well-read, and had a passion for the company of writers and intellectuals. One thing the two women had in common was that, though their husbands were thoroughly heterosexual, they themselves (being rather like Julia in this respect, or for that matter Carrington) delighted in the company of homosexual men. Rosamond was a great friend of Dadie Rylands, to whom she had dedicated her novel, and fell unrequitedly in love with the handsome Paul Cross, then having an affair with the teenager Angus Wilson (the future novelist). Diana – to the dismay of her husband, who worshipped her and would have liked to spend most of his time alone with her – revelled in the society of the brilliant (and mostly gay or bisexual) young men of Oxford's 'Brideshead generation', including Harold Acton, John Betjeman, Robert Byron, Brian Howard and Evelyn Waugh. In 1930, by which time both women had given birth to their first child (in each case a boy), the two couples went to live in beautiful houses not far from Ham Spray – Wogan and Rosamond rented the Jacobean Ipsden Manor in Oxfordshire, while Bryan and Diana bought the early Georgian Biddesden House in Wiltshire. By this time, both couples had become friends of Lytton and Carrington – Rosamond had got to know them through Dadie, while Diana had struck up an instant friendship with Lytton at a party of Lady Cunard's.

Meeting the two couples at Ham Spray, Tommy set out to enthrall them, with considerable success. Rosamond (who would subsequently come to regard Tommy as 'poisonous' and 'evil') admitted to Frances Partridge in the 1960s that she had 'fallen completely under the spell of his charm'. Wogan 'adored' him, and he often stayed (with or without Julia) as their guest at Ipsden – or went off rambling with Wogan, who shared his love of walking and talking.[179] In her memoirs, Diana writes that she 'saw a great deal' of Tommy and 'loved' him, adding that he was 'the best talker among the clever Bloomsburies [sic] I knew'.* She too enjoyed going for long walks with him – mostly in London, where she and Bryan had a house in Buckingham Gate.[180] Bryan, who was a rich man (unlike Wogan, whose family kept him on a tight financial rein), saw himself as a patron of the arts, and lost no time in adopting Tommy as his protégé. (A link already existed between them, as Bryan's chief mentor at Christ Church, Oxford had been Tommy's old friend Roy Harrod.) Tommy was commissioned to make busts of Diana and her infant son, and also to create a gigantic (eight feet tall) lead statue of a mother-earth figure ('Pomona'), to form the central point of a formal garden being designed at Biddesden, a project begun in 1931 but not completed until 1936.† As for Julia, both Rosamond and Diana liked her, finding her clever and funny. Meanwhile Wogan and Bryan (who while devoted to their wives often found themselves unable to resist the attractions of other women) were allured by Julia, who was flattered by their attentions, though at this stage her relations with them were merely flirtatious.

* 'His conversation', she added, 'had sustained brilliance, and did not rely on any trick of speech or paradox.'
† In fact Tommy never quite completed it: for some reason, 'he could not bring himself to turn the foremost knee of the statue' (though he had finished a terracotta maquette of the figure). In the end, the knee was 'turned' by Wogan. (Bryan Guinness, *Porpourri from the Thirties* [1982], pp. 60–1.)

Tommy's statue 'Pomona' in the garden at Biddesden

Around this time Tommy also saw much of two men, both relations of Julia, who confusingly were known by the same name – John Strachey. Evelyn John St Loe Strachey (1901–63) was the son of St Loe Strachey, owner and editor of the *Spectator*, who had given much work to Lytton (his third cousin) during his struggling early years as a writer. (St Loe had also employed Lytton's brother James as his private secretary, but sacked him owing to his pacifism in 1914.) This John had been a friend of both Eddy Sackville-West and Wogan Philipps at Eton and Oxford. Appalled at the plight of the working man at a time of unemployment, he became a prominent socialist journalist and was elected a Labour MP in 1929. He was Parliamentary Private Secretary to another fiery aristo-cratic young socialist, Sir Oswald Mosley, who served in Ramsay

Macdonald's Labour Government but resigned from it in impatience at its lack of radicalism, founding the New Party, which John joined (as did Wogan and Rosamond), but which failed to win a single seat at the 1931 general election. (Mosley went on to become a fascist, while both John and Wogan became communists.) Tommy often met him at Ipsden and engaged with him in fierce political discussions (though in common with most of Bloomsbury, Tommy was uninterested in party politics). This John was also well known to Julia, having been a lover of her great friend Hester Chapman. The other John, John Ralph Severs Strachey (1905–63), was Julia's first cousin, son of her Uncle Ralph who had worked as an engineer in India and died in 1923. He was a handsome, charming and feckless youth, described by his aunt Dorothy Bussy as 'an engaging creature … but too soft, too fluid, too unresisting ever to be able to achieve anything, I fear'.[181] He was happy to lead a pleasant, hedonistic life, largely financed by a succession of rich women. He became an artist and was a natural companion for Tommy, of whom he painted the indifferent but revealing portrait reproduced at the start of this chapter.

While these shared friendships added an extra dimension to the lives of Tommy and Julia, other factors continued to tear them apart. Julia's fear that living in London would exacerbate Tommy's drinking and other self-destructive habits proved well-founded. 'I got back here [to their flat in Arundel Gardens, Notting Hill] to find Tommy absolutely grey & haggard, [having been] dead drunk the night before, & in all sorts of trouble', she wrote to Carrington. 'I wish he'd stay in the country, he's much happier there.'[182] She consoled herself for her husband's neglect by having an affair with Gilbert Debenham,* brother of Helen Tomlin's friend Audrey, to

* Meeting him in London in the spring of 1929, Julia found him 'intelligent, witty, shy, excitable' (Frances Partridge, *Julia*, p. 113). The following year Tommy did a bust of him, which Carrington thought 'quite the best thing he has ever done' (Carrington to Lytton [BL]).

which Tommy (who seems to have held the view that he alone was entitled to engage in marital infidelity, indeed on a heroic scale) took violent exception. In the spring of 1931 Julia again departed on her own for a long and recuperative Mediterranean holiday with her aunt Dorothy Bussy at Roquebrune in the *Alpes-Maritimes*. The correspondence which she and Tommy exchanged during her absence has survived, and suggests that, though they still had affectionate feelings for one another, their relationship was wracking them both with guilt and unhappiness.

Julia to Tommy: Dearest Piggy, it was so perfectly awful seeing you cry at the boat… I'm just about to write to Gilbert the letter I said I would, saying I don't want to have any correspondence with him. I promise you faithfully I am going to be firm as a rock upon the point.

Tommy to Julia [*from Swallowcliffe*]: I must write to you if only to relieve the horror I am in. I want so terribly to be forgiven, and yet everything I think of saying seems to be making an excuse for myself and I do not believe there is any excuse. I think I am a most horrible cad, and no amount of explanation of why I am one or what it is like to be one can alter or improve the fact. I can't get the beastly business out of my head for a moment and the more I think of it the more nightmarish it seems. It now seems to me that if I had deliberately schemed to wound you and hurt you I could not have arranged it better. O my darling please please believe that though some horrible kink and madness takes hold of me, none of it appeared like this at the time. I only hope to God that, if I have made you unhappy, it is not quite as unhappy as I have made myself. If you were here I know you would be perfectly angelic and say, don't get in a stew. But I can't help it, it makes it worse your being so kind. Do, for God's sake, help. It's really all this drinking. I do so desperately want to make you happy and I do nothing but make you wretched. I will write to [Edward] Glover [his psychoanalyst]. I feel horribly ashamed.

Julia to Tommy: My darling and very dearest of Pigs, I have been in despair since I got your last letter… I think of you such a lot dearest, and wish I could comfort you and make you feel more happy.

Julia to Tommy: You ask me to tell you a little bit what I am thinking. I am feeling stunned, literally stunned after our awful time in England these last months. I feel sick, anxious, bewildered and absolutely muddled. I can't sleep and feel terribly guilty and miserable. And remorseful to the uttermost point… I'm in a nervous stew about what I call my physical complexes [presumably a reference to her basic dislike of sex]. I feel fussed and wretched about them – they have got to be dealt with somehow – but how? It's so terrible arguing about them together – as we used to; that is what I dread on my return to England… Goodbye, my dearest, dearest little pig. When you wake up in the night think that I am thinking of you.[183]

After Julia's return to England, they led a semi-detached married life, sometimes together in a London flat, sometimes accepting weekend invitations as a couple, often apart while one of them went to stay alone at Swallowcliffe, or with friends.

Any hopes Tommy may have had that the move to London would result in a stream of commissions were doomed to disappointment. In the world economic crisis resulting from the Wall Street Crash of October 1929 even the rich were more careful with their money, and most artists struggled. In fact, between the summers of 1930 and 1931, the only work he seems to have done (apart from the statue at Biddesden, and the 'china figures' referred to in the letters of Lytton and Carrington) are busts of his parents, no doubt commissioned by them as a way of helping him. They

Tommy's busts of his parents, 1930

are psychologically interesting. Lord Tomlin's head includes the heavily decorated collar of the privy counsellor uniform to which he had become entitled as a law lord. Together with his set lips, high forehead and deeply lined cheeks, this makes him appear grimly imposing and proconsular, the embodiment of the traditional 'establishment'. The bust may have been influenced by that of Asquith, the former prime minister, upon which Frank Dobson was working when Tommy was apprenticed to him in 1920–21. As for Lady Tomlin's portrait, to quote Oliver Garnett: 'With its rigidly frontal pose, closed eyes, and grimly set features, it resembles nothing so much as a death-mask ... all the more because the piece is considerably over life-size'.[184]

In the summer of 1931 Tommy partially realised an artistic ambition which he had harboured for some years – to make a portrait head of Virginia Woolf. He had first asked if she might consent to sit for him in December 1924 (as she recorded in her diary); but she was instinctively resistant to such a project. As her nephew and biographer Quentin Bell writes:

One of the things she most disliked in the world was being peered at... She didn't like being photographed, but if a painter or photographer is unwelcome, how much more so a sculptor? A sculptor has but one object: yourself – you from in front, you from behind, you from every conceivable angle – and his is a staring, measuring, twisting and turning business, an exhaustive and remorseless enquiry.[185]

Tommy enlisted Virginia's sister Vanessa as an ally, and finally it was agreed that Virginia would attend sittings at Tommy's studio in Percy Street, where she would be simultaneously sculpted by Tommy and sketched by Vanessa. The sessions began on 20 July. Virginia was a discontented sitter, and made an enormous fuss. On the third day, she wrote to Dorothy Bussy that

the man I hate most in the world, your nephew Tomlin, has me by the hair; I waste afternoon after afternoon perched in his rat-ridden and draught-riddled studio: can't escape. If I do,

Tommy's bust of Virginia, 1931: this copy sits opposite the site of her now demolished house in Tavistock Square

the bonds of friendship are (he says, and I wish it were true) torn asunder... Day after day thrown into the pit, and all for a woman's face.'*[186]

On the fourth day she wrote exasperatedly to Vanessa: 'Do you really think it is worth while for me to go on sitting? I'm quite prepared ... to sit until we go away, but I have a feeling that the bust won't conceivably be finished by then, and that the question of further sittings in the autumn will arise ... it would be sheer idiocy on my part to pretend that I can do this.'[187] A week later she wrote to her friend, the lesbian composer Ethyl Smyth, of the 'blessed relief of having done with sitting'. With some difficulty she was persuaded to return twice more in August. On 7 August she wrote in her diary:

> Then I sat to Tommie [sic]. Oh dear, what a terrific hemp strong heather root obstinate fountain of furious individuality shoots in me – they tampered with it, Nessa and Tommy – pinning me there, from 2 to 4 on 6 afternoons, to be looked at; I felt like a piece of whalebone bent ... I foamed with rage. T. was late. T. couldn't change his plans & so on. And I had to plod along the dusty street there.

After this, she declared that she would sit no more. Tommy (Oliver Garnett tells us) was 'disconsolate', but nevertheless had the head cast in its unfinished state.

Virginia hated the bust; and the whole episode ('when I took a shudder at the impact of his neurotic clinging persistency') led to an enduring chill in her relations with Tommy (though after his death she felt with a pang of remorse that she had 'behaved unreasonably, perversely').[188] Yet the semi-finished work is generally recognised as Tommy's masterpiece. To quote Quentin Bell:

* Virginia's letter indicates that this was intended to be a poetical allusion to 'Swift, if it was Swift'.

Stephen Tomlin's best claim to immortality rests upon that bust. It is not flattering. It makes Virginia look older and fiercer than she was. But it has a force, a life, a truth, which his other works ... do not possess. Virginia gave him no time to spoil his brilliant first conception. Irritated, despondent, reckless, he pushed his clay into position and was forced to give, while there was still time, the essential structure to her face. Her blank eyes stare as though in blind affronted dismay, but it is far more like than any of the photographs.[189]

Oliver Garnett adds: 'The head conveys not only dismay, but also the physical effects of the acute nervous exhaustion she was suffering from while sitting for it. For ... she was in the midst of correcting the final typescript and proofs of *The Waves*, and deep depression invariably overtook her when her novels reached these last stages of coming to press. The head makes such a stark and powerful impact because it manages to distil something of her feelings at the time'[190] – feelings to which Tommy, of course, was no stranger.

Virginia Woolf is not just Tommy's most famous (and arguably, his best) portrait head, but probably the last. After 1931 he seems to have done little sculpture: possibly his experience with Virginia set the seal on his disillusion with the medium (though he was still only thirty, and had been practising the craft for barely a decade). He continued to dabble in other art forms. One was theatrical design: he made a curtain for Clifford Bax's play *The Venetian*, which was performed at two London theatres in 1931, and contributed to the sets of other productions. And as will be seen in the next chapter, in his thirties he worked extensively in the field of decorative pottery, and wrote much melancholy poetry.

During the summer of 1931 – probably around the time he was trying to sculpt Virginia – Tommy met the person who was to become the chief companion of his remaining years. 'H.', as he was commonly known to all and sundry (his surname was probably

Tommy with 'H', photographed by Barbara Ker-Seymer through the legs of Wogan Philipps

Williams, though it has not so far been possible to discover what the initial 'H' represents), was a working-class youth from the Midlands, an unemployed hotel porter. Tommy picked him up at a cinema, took him home, and (presumably after some satisfactory sexual experiences) paid him to work as a model and assistant at his Percy Street studio. Carrington met him there, writing to Sebastian Sprott that he was 'a charming sweetie, very much your style – I couldn't help wishing I was Tommy!' Hearing his accent, she asked if he came from Nottingham, to be told: 'No, but it's strange you sa' that as I'm from Wolverhampton.' H., who had perky looks and a cheerful disposition, happily attached himself to Tommy, who by September had decided to officialise their association by employing H. as his manservant. (This was a common ploy in the case of a man from the 'higher orders' and a working-class youth living together, in those times when they could never be open about such relationships; Roger Senhouse similarly employed a batman named Peel, and around the time Tommy met H. the architect Montague Glover appointed his working-class lover Ralph Hall to be his chauffeur, the start of a relationship which would last more than fifty years.[191]) H.'s new role necessitated his learning how to cook; and Tommy appealed to Carrington, who was happy to assist, coming to stay with Tommy and H. in the 'dreary flat hundreds of miles away in Notting Hill' where Tommy and Julia were living (Julia being absent, as she often was). Carrington found the experience 'great fun' and in a few days trained H. to be 'a fine cook'. 'You wouldn't come out to a music hall tonight with Tommy and H.?', she wrote to Sebastian (having returned to her normal London abode in Bloomsbury). 'H. is a dream of a sweetie!'[192] Indeed, most of Tommy's friends liked H., who became (no doubt with Tommy's complicity) intimate with several of them, notably Duncan Grant and John Banting. Julia too accepted him: when, soon afterwards, she found an ideal (and mercifully inexpensive) flat in Wigmore Street, Marylebone, she wrote to Carrington that, if they moved there (it is not clear whether they ever did), they would have to rent an extra room nearby for H. When, during the autumn, Tommy went to stay at Ham Spray, H. accompanied him, being accommodated in the servants' quarters.

A letter survives from H. to Tommy, written during the last days of 1931 (when Tommy was staying with the Augustus Johns at Fryern). In a neat hand, it mostly concerns domestic matters – Mr Penrose has telephoned; the landlady of the studio wants to know when Tommy will be using it so she can heat it. H. wishes Tommy 'all the best for a brighter 1932', and concludes with a rather cheeky rhyme, alluding to two of his least favourite duties, to be sung to the tune of *Auld Lang Syne*:

> Now Tommy's gone away from here
> I'm happy as can be.
> No more setting of alarms
> Or early morning tea.

He signs himself 'Humble'.

Tommy remained close to his brother Garrow – though they did not see much of each other (except at the monthly dinners of the Cranium Club), or quite inhabit the same worlds. Garrow was now a busy London barrister, having reluctantly followed his father into the profession (and proved unexpectedly successful, with his pugnacious manner and quick mind). Unlike Tommy, he was a great sportsman, who loved to spend his leisure skiing, high-speed motoring (he once crashed his father's car) and yachting (he became a seafaring companion of Beakus Penrose). He was not invariably popular with Tommy's friends: Lytton thought him 'singularly lacking in charm' (and was unamused by his obsessive interest in flagellation);[193] Eddy found him a bore. On the other hand, he and Tommy had a common friend in Bunny Garnett.

Garrow (right) shortly before his death, with 'Beakus' Penrose (left)

Bunny had at first disliked Garrow, but witnessed an extraordinary transformation in him during the 1920s. 'From being an unhappy, self-centred and aggressive egoist, he became sunny and unselfish. His behaviour towards women was transformed also, and soon he became the kind of man whom they could trust and love.' He frequently stayed at Hilton, where he 'did not inspire the devotion generally felt for Tommy, but was always a welcome visitor'.[194]

We have an interesting account of Garrow in the memoirs of Alix Kilroy (who later married Francis Meynell, Bunny's partner in the Nonesuch Press, and as Dame Alix Meynell became one of the leading civil servants of her generation). Alix was a shy and innocent Oxford undergraduate when she met Garrow on a skiing holiday in Switzerland during the winter of 1924–5. She was both fascinated and terrified by this muscular giant with his hearty manner and air of worldliness, who could not keep his hands off her. Back in England, they kept in touch, and met periodically; but it was not until 1929, when she was twenty-six and he, thirty-one, that she – still a virgin – finally succumbed to his advances. Garrow told her that he regarded sex as 'a pleasant and natural part of friendship' – in which respect he resembled both Tommy and Bunny. But he also warned the unfortunate woman (who had secretly worshipped him ever since setting eyes on him) that he wanted no emotional involvement with her; that, if she were so foolish as to fall in love with him, he would wash his hands of her; that it was his habit to have several women on the go at any time, and that there was no question of his marrying any of them. Tortured by a passion which she struggled to conceal, she accepted these conditions for their affair and endured various humiliations (such as his seducing her flatmate when the three of them spent the weekend together). She tells us two other things about Garrow. Like Tommy, he loved talking – but whereas Tommy sought to guide the conversation to the subjects which interested his interlocutor, Garrow was in the habit of lecturing the company on matters concerning which he was knowledgeable and the others ignorant. And like Tommy, Garrow suffered from 'black depressions': he explained to Alix (as Tommy did to Julia) that this was a 'kink' over which he had no control. For a time he underwent psychoanalysis (possibly with Tommy's analyst, Edward Glover); but he finally gave this up, concluding that his condition was 'hopeless and incurable'.[195]

In the late 1920s Bunny, inspired by his new friend T. E. Lawrence, became a keen aviator. He suggested to Garrow that he too take up flying, which Garrow did in 1931, joining a flying club at Nazeing near Broxbourne in Hertfordshire. Bunny now looked upon Garrow (who was thirty-three) as a perfect specimen of manhood. 'He was in such perfect health, so physically radiant, that he spread happiness wherever he went... The rugged face with its watchful grey eyes, the cap of naturally waved hair rippling back from his forehead, his broad chest, his great muscular strength – everything revealed a splendid man *flowering...*' On one of Garrow's visits to Hilton they tried out 'a test for liability to giddiness as a pilot', which involved holding a walking stick upright, putting one's nose to the handle, and walking round it three times with one's eyes shut. Bunny passed the test, being able to walk straight once he opened his eyes, but Garrow 'staggered helplessly about'. They just laughed. It was with horror that, on 14 December that year, Bunny learned that Garrow had been killed the previous afternoon when, taking his aircraft out of a right-hand spin, he unintentionally put it into an uncontrollable left-hand spin at low altitude, leading to an inevitable crash. Bunny was consumed by guilt: not only had he been responsible for Garrow's learning to fly, but following the walking-stick experiment he should have warned him 'that any kind of aerobatics might be fatal to him'.[196]

Garrow's death came to Tommy as a shattering blow. He lost a beloved brother; and the tragedy served to intensify the strains within the Tomlin family (including the mutual antipathy which existed between Julia and Tommy's sister Joan). 'It has been so awful & gloomy', wrote Julia to Carrington.

> Tommy is so upset. And the Judge had to go down to the scene of action, poor old neurotic father that he is. Lady T. is now taking the line that G. was the perfect son, & speaks of him as though they had been bosom pals & so friendly together always. Joan Trower apparently rushed into Garrow's rooms [in Great James Street, Soho] first thing this morning before anyone else in order to 'put everything to rights' & be very practical and businesslike. Next, Tom Trower seemed to think that he was the only person qualified to deal with Garrow's papers, & Tommy had to elbow his way in to get a chance of being allowed to express *his* opinion on Garrow's affairs or take any part at all. Tom Trower's only idea has been to confiscate *The Psychology of Sex* [by Havelock Ellis] which he found on G's bookshelf, & hide it away, also the book of nude photographs... We are getting along as well as can be expected, with the aid of whiskeys & sodas, aspirins & bromides. But the question of whether Tommy will be expected to appear at the cremation service down at Ash in Kent is the real horror now looming. Helen & I are doing all we can to fight against the whole notion. It is *too* awful to have to go & hang about over a brother's ashes & sing hymns in a body of weeping relatives. Uncle Jimmy [the Judge's clergyman younger brother, now a Canon of Canterbury Cathedral] is choosing favourite hymns for the occasion, & telephoning to London all the time to ask if his choice is approved of.

However, in her next letter, Julia reported that the event had passed off satisfactorily. 'Tommy got through the funeral better than expected yesterday, thank God, & he is all right... A lot of people turned up at Ash which pleased the relations very much. There was a splendid sort of gents' beauty chorus of young barristers from Lincoln's Inn in top hats who stamped around in a crocodile formation.'

Lytton, towards
the end of his
life, gazes ador-
ingly at Tommy
in the garden at
Ham Spray: the
woman on the
left of the picture
is Reine Pitman,
and the head of
Saxon Sydney-
Turner is visible
between Tommy
and Lytton

Augustus and Dorelia John invited Tommy and Julia to spend Christmas with them at Fryern; but for the festival itself they were obliged to stay with Tommy's family at Bengeo Hall, the Trowers' house near Hertford. 'It seems that Joan is trying to turn over a new leaf & make friends with Tommy again', wrote Julia to Carrington. 'Very charming and laudable – but oh what trouble it is going to lead us into in the future!' On Boxing Day they joined the Johns' Christmas house party (which apart from Augustus's numerous children included his new son-in-law, the charismatic scientist and jockey Derek Jackson, and the artist Adrian Daintrey), an environment which provided some relaxation after a traumatic fortnight.

Tommy was given little respite, however, for almost immediately he was caught up in a new tragic drama. Lytton, who had been feeling increasingly unwell since mid-November, was now gravely and mysteriously ill at Ham Spray. (He was in fact suffering from stomach cancer, too advanced to admit of any treatment – though this was never diagnosed by any of the eminent specialists who came to examine him.) Although, for the previous five years, Lytton had been in love with Roger Senhouse, he remained deeply fond of

Tommy, who continued to regard him as a beloved father figure: only a few months earlier, Tommy had been distraught at the thought (which proved unfounded) that he had offended Lytton for some reason.* Before the year was out, Tommy had made the first of several mercy missions to Lytton's bedside, being one of the few friends the ailing writer wished to see.[197] But Lytton grew visibly weaker by the day, and as none of the treatments prescribed by the doctors proved effective, it did not seem that he could survive much longer. The concern of those closest to him was concentrated on Carrington, who had often declared that she could not live without Lytton, and that if he died, she would take her own life. This further catastrophe had to be prevented somehow.

At Carrington's request, Gerald Brenan joined the small group of friends congregating at Ham Spray. According to Gerald's memoirs,

* On 27 June 1931, Lytton wrote to Roger that 'Tommy rang me up … to ask whether for some unknown reason I was absolutely enraged with him! My look the night before had struck such dread and horror into his soul… I was able to reassure him… He comes down today [to Ham Spray] for the week-end, which I shall enjoy very much.' (Berg Collection.)

Ralph (who despite his now longstanding affair with Frances continued to feel responsible for Carrington as her husband) confided to him that, as soon as Lytton's death seemed imminent,

> he would send for Tommy, who had already been warned and was standing by … [for] he was certain that, while Tommy was in the house, Carrington would not take her life. It was a cruel expedient, for its efficacy depended on Tommy being so unbalanced and neurotic, so shattered by his brother's recent death, so prone himself to suicide, with his marriage to Julia Strachey, which Carrington had arranged, on the point of breaking down and all his supports in life tottering, that Carrington's sense of responsibility would be aroused and she would pull herself together to look after him. In addition to this there would be the shock to him of Lytton's death. Lytton was one of his most intimate friends and in his close relations with other people there was always a strong element of dependence. But in order to come to this decision Ralph had had to overcome his own prejudices. Jealous of every man who showed signs of being attracted either to Carrington or to Frances, he had some time before conceived an aversion for Tommy. However in this emergency he decided to overlook this.

On 20 January, it was clear that Lytton's end was near, and Ralph duly summoned Tommy, asking Gerald to meet him at the station. Gerald's account continues:

> Tommy stepped out of the train looking more than usually pale and undecided and we set off in silence to Ham Spray. But Carrington, though apparently glad to see him, would not hear of his staying in the house, so I took him back to the Bear Inn at Hungerford. Here a party of Stracheys was assembled, but they went off almost at once to bed while Tommy and I sat up talking and drinking till two in the morning. We had been on

somewhat distant terms for several years, but at Garrow's funeral had come together and now I found his company very welcome. So many thoughts and feelings had accumulated in my mind that I was glad to have a person as intelligent and perceptive as he was to air them with. When at last we went upstairs he asked if he could sleep in my room since he could not face the idea of spending the night alone. I said, 'Yes, of course,' but then instead of lying down in the spare bed, to my embarrassment he got into my double one and burst into tears. It was impossible not to be touched by his misery and I regretted that I was not a young woman to be able to console him more effectively.[198]

At six o'clock that morning Carrington did try to kill herself, by shutting herself in the garage with the car exhaust running; only the chance fact that Lytton suddenly took a turn for the worse, and the household, woken by the nurse, started searching for her, prevented her succeeding. Tommy was immediately fetched in the

Ralph Partridge with Tommy – no love lost

belief that his presence would discourage her from making another attempt. In the course of the morning, everyone said goodbye to Lytton, who allegedly produced the farewell remark that 'if this is dying, I don't think much of it'. In the early afternoon, attended by his brothers Oliver and James, his sister Philippa, and Carrington and Ralph, he breathed his last, aged fifty-one. Tommy did not intrude upon this family scene: looking out of the window just after Lytton's death, Carrington saw him 'outside ... in the sunshine, walking backwards and forwards picking dead sticks up off the lawn'.[199]

In accordance with his plan, Ralph had Tommy move into Ham Spray – where Tommy stayed, joined at times by Julia, for the next five weeks. Employing all his talent for argument and persuasion, and invoking the love they had borne for each other and the sufferings they had both recently undergone, Tommy urged Carrington to carry on and face the future. Although she remained in a state of misery, his ministrations were effective at least in postponing the evil day. As she wrote in the journal into which she continued to pour her feelings and thoughts: 'He persuaded me that after a serious operation or fever, a man's mind would not be in a good state to decide on such an important step ... so I will defere [sic] my decision for a month or two until the result of the operation is less acute.'[200] At the end of January she wrote to him that 'you made this last week bearable which nobody else could have done. Those endless conversations were not quite pointless.'[201] She was also consoled by his reading poetry to her, especially the Elizabethan verse Lytton had loved. When Julia came, she wrote to Ralph (who had gone away for a few days with Frances): 'I have good news of Carrington. She seems thoroughly interested in whatever conversation is going forward, talks a lot, makes jokes, eats and sleeps. Tommy tells me she is definitely getting better all the time now.'[202] As February progressed, Carrington felt well enough to visit the Johns at Fryern and the Guinnesses at

Biddesden, and accepted a proposal of Dorelia John that they go on a trip to France together in mid-March. Gerald considered it essential that Tommy continue to 'guard' her up to the moment of departure; but by the end of February, Ralph had had enough of Tommy, whose job, he felt, had been done, and asked him to leave. Tommy did not object to this dismissal: the strain of the past weeks had been terrible, and he longed to get away.[203]

On the morning of 11 March, three days before she was due to leave for France with Dorelia, Carrington, who was alone at Ham Spray, shot herself with a gun she had borrowed from Biddesden, claiming she wanted it for shooting rabbits. A tearful Tommy went round to Bloomsbury to break the news to Leonard and Virginia, and other members of the set. In her farewell letter to Ralph, Carrington asked that Tommy be paid £100 to design her tombstone – but Ralph suppressed this request:[204] no doubt he was motivated in part by jealousy, but as he now intended to marry Frances and live with her at Ham Spray (as Carrington in her letter indeed urged him to do), he felt that a visible local memorial to his late wife would be out of place. In the event, her ashes were scattered at an unrecorded spot, probably in the garden.

Tommy's portrait by Henry Lamb, 1932

VIII

DISINTEGRATION

1932–1937

Within the space of three months, Tommy had lost a beloved brother to an appalling accident, an adulated father-figure to an agonising illness, and a dear friend to suicide (the threat of which had kept him in a state of anguish for weeks). Prone as he was to moods of despair, he found himself plunged into the blackest depression, and experienced (to use a term then fashionable) a nervous breakdown. After a few months, he seems to have made a partial recovery. He and H. joined Wogan on a walking holiday in Provence, which helped restore his equilibrium.*[205] He sat to Henry Lamb for a portrait, which shows him looking fat, ravaged and far older than his thirty-one years, but nevertheless suggests that he had recovered his sparkle. Yet he was never quite the same. He had lost such ambition and motivation he had once possessed. He appears to have done no more original work as a sculptor (and could not even bring himself to complete the gigantic statue at Biddesden, though a full-size terracotta model he had made of it featured in an exhibition at the Burlington Galleries in 1935[206]). He increasingly abandoned himself to an aimless bohemian life.

For the rest of 1932–33, Tommy lived in a *ménage à trois* with

---

* They were accompanied on this trip by John Strachey – though it is not clear whether this was the politician or the artist, both of whom Tommy and Wogan knew well. (The politician, who like Wogan was converting to communism at that time, was also experiencing some psychological trauma, owing to the collapse both of his political career and his marriage.)

Tommy with the model of
'Pomona' at the Burlington
Galleries, 1935

Julia and H. – though Julia was often absent. Having resumed her
old friendship with Frances Marshall, she generally spent her weekends at Ham Spray, where Frances, who married Ralph Partridge
in 1933, was now mistress of the house: it annoyed Tommy that
she was now a more welcome visitor there than he. Professionally,
Tommy occupied himself with an activity which, while less
demanding, both physically and emotionally, than sculpture, was
reasonably remunerative and gave some scope to his artistic talents
– the making of decorative ceramics. This came about through
his friendship with the potter Phyllis Keyes (1882–1961), a woman
old enough to be his mother. Phyllis came from an old military
family: her brother, Admiral Sir Roger (later Baron) Keyes, then
commanded the Fleet at Portsmouth. Tommy got to know her
when she set up her kiln in Warren Street, round the corner from
Percy Street where he had his studio. Although she lived for some
years in a lesbian relationship, she was (like many of the women in
this story) attracted to homosexual and bisexual men. She fell in
love with Duncan Grant, to the point that Vanessa had to write to

Two of Tommy's ceramic artefacts

her warning that nothing could come of the infatuation.[207] At all events, she became extremely friendly with both Tommy and H., who were henceforth closely involved in her work. Phyllis produced decorative items – some of original design, others copied from traditional Mediterranean pottery – which were hand-painted by various artists (including Duncan and Vanessa) before being finished with a distinctive milky-white tin glaze. Originally, Tommy helped design her pottery, but by the time she moved from Warren Street to a larger workshop in nearby Clipstone Street, he had become her partner, involved in all stages of production: the artefacts they created bore their joint cyphers, Phyllis's 'crossed-keys' symbol and Tommy's monogram. (When, after Tommy's death, Bunny visited the workshop, he was surprised to discover 'a lot of stuff I had never seen before'.[208]) Tommy also did occasional

Phyllis Keyes's 'crossed-keys' cypher and Tommy's 'ST' monogram

Barbara
Ker-Seymer

work during the 1930s for his old teacher Frank Dobson: at the
time of his death, he was helping Dobson design the Canadian
Pavilion for the British Industries Fair.[209]

At some point in 1932, while Tommy was absent from London,
Julia accepted a part-time job as assistant to the photographer
Barbara Ker-Seymer at her studio in Grafton Street, Mayfair. '£1 a
week, plus commissions', she wrote to Tommy. 'It will help me get
up in the mornings.'[210] The elegant and alluring Barbara (1905–93)
was then enjoying a brief vogue, with portraits in *Tatler* and
Harper's Bazaar, but was no conventional society photographer,
having been strongly influenced by the kitsch and surrealism of
late Weimar German photography. Her principal artistic mentors
were the outrageously homosexual John Banting and Brian

Two portraits of
Tommy by Barbara

A rare photograph of Tommy in playful mood, taken by Barbara

Howard, both friends of Tommy and Julia. She was yet another woman who enjoyed the society of gay men – though she herself was heterosexual and had numerous lovers, including Wogan, Bunny, Beakus, Ralph Partridge, John Strachey (the artist, not the politician), and Tommy himself.[211] Tommy, indeed, became one of her great friends: he often features in her photograph albums, and there was even a suggestion that they might live together.* A constant party seems to have gone on around her, involving copious quantities of sex, drugs and booze, in which Tommy intermittently participated for the rest of his life.

---

* On 11 September 1933, Ralph Partridge wrote to her: 'I must have invented it, or did you say you might set up with Tommy?' (Ker-Seymer papers, Tate Gallery.)

Julia had now finished the novella she had written during her French holidays: she submitted it to Virginia Woolf at the Hogarth Press, who thought it 'astonishingly good' and agreed to take it.[212] It was published as *Cheerful Weather for the Wedding* in September 1932, with a dust jacket designed by Duncan Grant (Virginia had originally invited Carrington to design it, when she visited her at Ham Spray on the eve of Carrington's suicide). It is set on a blustery March afternoon at a country house on the Dorset coast, where the eldest daughter is being married to an English diplomat. Outwardly it is a comedy, featuring eccentric relations, dotty servants, naughty schoolboys, guests put into the wrong bedrooms. Underlying the comic narrative, however, is a dark sense of unease – and indeed it turns out that the situation is tragic, for this is a loveless marriage forced on the bride by the fact that, a year earlier, she had become pregnant outside wedlock, a nightmare from which she extricated herself by bearing the child abroad and having it adopted locally (possibly with the connivance of the man she is now marrying). To add to the discomfort of the wedding party, the father of the abandoned child is present in a state of some hysteria, tormented by the thought that he should have married the bride himself when he had the chance. Presiding over the scene is the absurd figure of the bride's mother, Mrs Thatcham, a woman who tries to avoid all the problems and unpleasantnesses of life by focussing on trivialities and remaining resolutely cheerful. Julia (we are told by Frances Partridge) based Mrs Thatcham on her mother-in-law, Lady Tomlin.[213] *Cheerful Weather* was well-received, and seemed to mark the start of a promising literary career – but the lazy and disorganised Julia produced nothing more for publication during the 1930s. (The novella has been much reprinted down the years, and a film adaptation, produced by Donald Rice, was released in 2011.)

In May 1933 it was Tommy's turn to appear (albeit anonymously) in print, when a long poem he had written was published in the

New Statesman and Nation under the title *The Sluggard's Quadrille, by the Lobster* (reproduced as Appendix III). This alludes to *The Lobster Quadrille*, a piece of nonsense verse in Chapter 10 of *Alice's Adventures in Wonderland*, which is recited partly by the Mock Turtle, partly by Alice herself. The portion recited by Alice in turn alludes to a seventeenth-century moralistic poem, *The Sluggard* by Isaac Watts (which warns against the dangers of leading an idle and unproductive life), and concerns a lobster which claims to be carefree, but is in fact terrified of sharks. *The Sluggard's Quadrille* contains allusions to many other literary sources, including Shakespeare, Coleridge, Wordsworth, Tennyson and the Bible. While on one level it is a piece of rollicking and ingenious doggerel, it has a nightmarish quality. At night, the poet finds himself swept out to sea, where he experiences all kinds of terrors, including sharks and other monsters, the prospect of drowning, the sight of dry land flooding and disappearing. He finds himself drifting helplessly from the familiar shore; he strives to reach the further shore, only to find it does not exist. In the water, he finds himself utterly alone and surrounded by filth. With daybreak, he awakes from the nightmare:

> Then to my heart a hope returns
> And once again the spirit burns!

But he knows that he will again have to face the horror:

> It is a dreadful thing for me
> To find myself each night – at Sea.

He longs for the call of 'Time, Gentlemen' (the traditional cry of the pub landlord at closing time), so he can reach

> The tideless ocean of the grave …
> Where shafts of dawn no more will prise
> The unwilling shutters of the eyes.

The literary editor of the *New Statesman* was Bunny Garnett, who considered that *The Sluggard's Quadrille* was 'one of the most tragic poems of despair in the English language', and the most important thing he published during his years in the post.[214] He considered Tommy a poet of the first rank, and lamented (both during Tommy's lifetime and after his death) that, though constantly scribbling ingenious verse, he never preserved enough of it to fill a volume for publication.[215]

The Sluggard's Quadrille shows that Tommy, though still able to demonstrate impressive creative gifts at the age of thirty-two, remained in a dark and depressed state; and in this mood, the demonic side of his nature inevitably predominated. Frances Partridge once referred to Tommy's 'desire to conquer and wreck',[216] and his influence upon the marriage of Wogan and Rosamond during the years 1932–4 is a case in point. Wogan loved Rosamond dearly: they had endured much struggle and sacrifice in order to marry, as at the time they fell in love Rosamond was married to someone else. There were two problems, however: Wogan had a roving eye, and could not help falling for other women; and he was temperamentally ill-suited to the domestic life to which Rosamond was bound as the mother of their two small children. He sought the advice of Tommy, whom he (not being especially bright) looked up to as a fount of wisdom. Tommy advised him to follow Oscar Wilde's dictum that 'the only way to deal with a temptation is to yield to it'; to have affairs with any women he fancied; and to use his career as an artist to stay away from home (and from Rosamond) as much as possible. As Wogan later wrote to Rosamond: 'He became my father confessor … [and] made me give up all hope of you & me ever becoming right.'[217] By the time she received this letter, Rosamond was well aware of Tommy's malignity towards her: she had been dancing with him at a party and telling him how much she liked him when he stopped, looked at her coldly, and said: 'You do, do you? Well, you'd better not, because I'm

Tommy photographed by Barbara at Ipsden (the house visible in the background) on a visit to Wogan (Rosamond presumably being absent) in July 1934

doing all I can to break up your marriage.'[218] As the marriage deteriorated (though it staggered on uneasily for the rest of the 1930s), Rosamond placed much of the blame upon Tommy, whom she denounced as 'poisonous',[219] 'evil',[220] and 'complicated, abnormal, a bad influence'.[221] In fact, owing to her pathological possessiveness, all Rosamond's relationships with the men in her life were doomed to ultimate disaster – but Tommy certainly behaved in this case, as no doubt in others, with cruelty and malevolence.

Another marriage which broke down was that of Bryan and Diana Guinness, Diana having, during the summer of 1932, fallen madly (and requitedly) in love with Sir Oswald Mosley, then transforming himself from a socialist into a fascist. She faced a difficult decision, as Mosley was then married to Lady Cynthia Curzon (who would conveniently die the following year); by leaving Bryan to live with Mosley she would therefore find herself in a social limbo, cut off from respectable society and to some extent from her two small sons. By the end of 1932 she had made her choice to leave her husband and follow her new lover, wherever this might take her. Did she consult Tommy about her predicament? We know that he and Diana were still going for long walks together in London as late as November 1932 (as Diana recalled in her memoirs that, during one of these excursions, he expressed satisfaction at Hitler's disappointing performance in that month's German elections). Bryan, who was plunged into misery by Diana's desertion, does seem to have sought the counsel of Tommy, who urged him to try psychoanalysis (advice which Bryan, observing the effect it appeared to have had on Tommy himself, decided to ignore).[222]

The oddest aspect of all this is that, once Wogan had accepted Tommy's advice to follow his amorous inclinations, and Bryan, deserted by Diana, sought consolation elsewhere, they both, in the course of 1933, had affairs with Julia. Julia did not in fact enjoy sex, and her diary suggests that she found the physical attentions of both men unwelcome;[223] but such was her yearning for the affection which they clearly both felt for her, and which had generally been denied to her by Tommy, that she yielded to their advances. At the same time, remembering Tommy's violent reaction on discovering her affair with Gilbert Debenham, she wished to keep the knowledge of these relationships (both with men he regarded as friends) from Tommy for as long as possible. As Frances Partridge wrote in her diary:

> When [Julia] stayed [at Ham Spray] at the end of August [1933] she told me about her affair with Wogan Philipps. At first he was the ardent wooer and Julia held back a little. Then they spent a week in Weymouth together and he was so charming that she fell very much in love with him and he with

her. Wogan felt he must tell Rosamond, but Tommy had not been told. He [Tommy] clutched on to Julia as his last hope, in an almost lunatic way and can't bear that his marriage should appear to the world as a failure – this in spite of the fact that he beds with all and sundry, with the exception of Julia for some time past. She longs for a complete parting but dare not take the responsibility, nor let him discover about Wogan. Also Wogan is devoted to Tommy.[224]

But although Tommy was not told, he seems to have guessed. As Wogan wrote to Julia when, following one of their secret assignations, he ran into Tommy: 'It was like seeing a Dante-esque ghost. How ill he looked. And the hostility in his "hullo". I am so terribly fond of him & long to do something for him, & his appearance & hostility were a ghastly shock.'[225]

Meanwhile, Tommy's relations with Julia were going from bad to worse. The tragedy was that part of him still loved her and could not bear the thought of her leaving him. But the moments when he expressed such feelings for her became ever rarer, while his general behaviour towards her became ever more abusive and sadistic.[226] Finally, early in 1934, she made up her mind to leave him. She later wrote to Bryan that this was her third attempt in three years to do so, the previous ones having been thwarted by his threats of suicide.[227] The occasion for their parting was Julia's acceptance of an invitation from Frances and Ralph to join them on a winter holiday in Portugal. It was arranged that, after their departure, friends of Tommy, including Julia's father Oliver, as well as Tommy's psychoanalyst Edward Glover, would explain to him that she would not be rejoining him on her return as she required a period of separation. Much to the relief of all concerned, Tommy received this news calmly.[228] During her Portuguese holiday, Julia ran into Gamel Woolsey, an American poetess who had for some years been the lover of Llewellyn Powys, and who would shortly marry Gerald Brenan. Gamel wrote to Llewellyn that she liked Julia, whom she pitied for having endured 'a really horrid life with Stephen Tomlin, with his general shiftlessness, his drink and his drugs and his lower class young men'.[229] On her return to London in March, Julia moved into a small house in Weymouth Street, Marylebone, which she henceforth shared with Frances and Ralph. Tommy, while respecting her desire to remain apart from him, begged her not to leave him irrevocably, and she agreed to delay her decision for six months – though at the end of that time, in late 1934, she asked for a formal separation. One result of this was that Tommy's father promptly reduced the allowance he paid his son on the supposition that he no longer had to maintain a wife[*] – though as Julia had few financial resources of her own, and Tommy insisted on continuing to share with her such money as he had, his financial plight became acute.[230] Divorce, though recommended by Lord Tomlin's son-in-law and solicitor Tom Trower (whom Julia disliked and hated dealing with), never seems to have been seriously considered by either Tommy or Julia, presumably because they both wished to avoid the expense and public scandal, and (during the remainder of Tommy's life) neither of them had it in mind to marry anyone else.

Tommy could still rely on the fidelity and companionship of H., with whom he lived, following the separation from Julia, at 8 Percy Street (where their landlady, Miss Pritchard, seems to have become quite fond of them, and presumably gave them more of the house to live in than the original 'rat-ridden and draught-riddled studio' which had so disgusted Virginia in 1931). In the summer of 1934, they had a holiday together at some location which (so Wogan wrote to Barbara) they enjoyed so much that they thought of

---

* Julia wrote to Frances (March 1935) that her father-in-law was reducing the allowance 'by £300' – but this is probably a slip for 'to £300' (which was still a decent sum to live on in 1935, representing the salary which, for example, James Lees-Milne was paid when engaged as Country Houses Secretary of the National Trust a year later).

returning there (it is not clear where) for good.[231] Once, when
Tommy went away without him, H. wrote to him from Percy
Street: 'Tommy, don't stop away too long, I miss you such a lot
these days, when I'm depressed there's no one to talk to and when
I'm happy there's no one to be happy with.'[232] But by the spring of
1935 even H. was finding the experience of living with Tommy
insupportable, and he moved out into lodgings of his own. In
May 1935 Duncan wrote to Vanessa that he had been to the cinema
with H. who was 'really charming and amusing' and had 'made
it up with Tommy, so that seems all right'.[233] They remained good
friends, it seems, so long as they did not live under the same roof.
(After Tommy's death, Duncan would keep an eye on H. and look
after him, helping him find work and advancing him money,
which H. usually repaid.[234]) In May 1936 Tommy and H. were both
present at a cocktail party given by Phyllis in Clipstone Street,
at which unglazed ashtrays were put out together with paints and
brushes for the guests to decorate.[235]

The only member of his family to whom Tommy remained
close was his sister Helen. (She had exclaimed on hearing of
Garrow's death: 'Thank God it wasn't Tommy.'[236]) She had fallen
in love with Frank Goldby (1903–97), a university lecturer in medicine who shared her interest in archaeology. The son of a humble
pharmacist, he was disapproved of by her parents, who considered
him a fortune hunter.[237] In the autumn of 1932 Helen and Frank
left England and married in Hong Kong, where he had been
offered a teaching position. The marriage was happy, resulting
in six children. Frank was subsequently elected to a Cambridge
fellowship, spent the war in Australia, and ended his career as
Professor of Anatomy at St Mary's Hospital, London.

Tommy continued to join the annual summer family reunions
at Upper Hardres where he was as popular as ever with his Trower
nephews, who delighted in his company without ever being aware
of the problems in his life. It was during one of these summer

gatherings, in August 1935, that Tommy's father suddenly died at a Canterbury nursing home, of peritonitis following an operation for appendicitis. He was sixty-eight, and still active as a judge.* Apart from a few legacies to servants, he bequeathed his entire estate to his widow; had she predeceased him, his will dated 25 August 1932 provided that the bulk of his property should pass to his elder daughter Joan, only a small share going to Tommy and Helen, with elaborate safeguards to ensure they could only touch the income and not the capital. (As Lord Tomlin explained in the will, his younger children had already received most of their share of the inheritance during his lifetime.) Julia was sorry to learn that Tommy, his last remaining son, would not inherit his title (as a law lord he only had a life peerage), and was relieved to know that, although she would not become Lady Tomlin, she and her estranged husband at least remained 'Honourables'.[238]

It is likely that the death of a parent with whom he had always had difficult relations and to whom he had never become reconciled further depressed Tommy's spirits. For some time he had been going steadily downhill, drowning himself in alcohol and no longer even seeing much of his old friends. Such mentions as they made of him in their letters mostly refer to alcoholic debauches: when he joined a house party in Dorset in September 1934 of Lord ('Naps') Allington, Wogan wrote to Barbara Ker-Seymer that he 'looked desperate', insulted the women present and 'resorted heavily to the whisky bottle'.[239] During his twenties, Tommy had to some extent moved between two worlds, the elegant upper-middle-class world and the devil-may-care bohemian world ('Bloomsbury' containing elements of both); but he now had little connection with

---

* As a judge, Lord Tomlin is particularly remembered for two things: the 'Tomlin Orders', still used to give effect to out-of-court settelements; and his judgment in the Duke of Westminster's case (1931), which established the principle (since overturned) that no one is liable for a tax unless their actions fall strictly within the terms of the relevant statute.

the former. As Virginia put it, he had 'deserted the respectable'.[240] When Roy Harrod invited him to dine at his Oxford college, Tommy regretfully had to decline as he no longer possessed a dinner jacket.[241] (The same problem no doubt prevented him from attending receptions at the American Embassy, where his old flame Henrietta Bingham now presided as hostess, her father having been appointed Ambassador by Roosevelt in 1933.) From time to time he tried to start a new life, either in the country or abroad; but such experiments never lasted long. ('He seemed depressed at the thought of going abroad which he says he hates', wrote Vanessa to Duncan, 'chiefly I think because when he doesn't know the language conversation is restricted. However he hoped that making a break now may cure him of his drinking habits.'[242]) The friend with whom he most often stayed was Beakus Penrose, at his house near Truro in Cornwall: accompanied by Barbara, he spent Christmas 1934 there, delighting the village children with his performance as Father Christmas.[243] He also revisited Chaldon for the first time in some years – he had been inhibited from going there by Sylvia's presence (she and her partner Valentine lived in the village from 1930 to 1934), and by Theo's dislike of Julia; the infant girl whom Theo and his wife Violet adopted in 1934 later remembered him, wearing a flowing red kerchief, carrying her over the downs to the cliffs.[244]

In fact, during 1935 and 1936, Tommy rarely seems to have strayed far from 'Fitzrovia', the busy, somewhat shabby district bounded by Euston Road in the north, Tottenham Court Road in the east, Oxford Street in the south and Great Portland Street in the west, which was known from the 1870s to the 1950s as a haunt of artists, writers, musicians and bohemians. Phyllis had her workshop there, and Duncan and Vanessa their studios; apart from H., he had many friends in the neighbourhood, including John Banting and John Strachey (the artist). He became a well-known character in local pubs such as the Fitzroy Tavern, the Bricklayers

Arms, the Wheatsheaf (apparently his favourite) and the Marquess of Granby – all of which had something of a reputation as homosexual pick-up joints. (Virginia once declared that 'Tommy can't make a story out of life, for all his sitting in pubs'; Vanessa disagreed.[245]) He was no doubt acquainted with other frequenters of these hostelries, from seasoned denizens such as the artist Nina Hamnett (1890–1956) to recent arrivals such as the poet Dylan Thomas (1914–53), though there is scant evidence of their encounters.* He was also a regular customer at the Eiffel Tower, a fashionable restaurant a few doors from his lodgings in Percy Street: it was an expensive establishment, but the exuberant Viennese-Jewish owner, Rudolf Stulick, seems to have extended Tommy unlimited credit, partly out of affection, partly because he brought richer friends to eat there.[246] Sometimes (though increasingly rarely) he crossed Tottenham Court Road into smarter Bloomsbury to visit his old friends Virginia and Leonard Woolf, Maynard and Lydia Keynes, Adrian and Karin Stephen, James and Alix Strachey. He wrote much indifferent poetry, generally on the themes of hopelessness and longing for death.

> Let us forget that we had honour ever;
> Let us forget that we were ever glad.
> Mock me no more, my soul, with hope we had,
> Cheat not despair with vain, with more endeavour.
> Droop, wingéd head! Your wingéd sandals sever.
> Why did you join with the corrupting clay,
> So fleet and fine, to cast yourself away
> In filthy, fleshy den to die forever?
> [Using] my strength and you, O soul, the lever,
> We did conspire to prise the Heavenly door;

---

* In an unreliable volume of memoirs published just before her death, *Is She a Lady?* (1955), Nina describes being taken to a fancy dress party by John Banting where she was plied with drinks by a solicitous man then unknown to her, later identified as Tommy, and the host.

But you are brought, sweet flyer, to the floor,
Pulled down by me to perish in my fever.
Fair flame and filthy tallow! At day's brink
Tallow and flame must both go out in stink.[*]

In December 1936 (the month Edward VIII gave up the throne
to marry the woman he loved) Tommy was staying with the Johns
at Fryern. It was an anxious time for Augustus, who was preoccupied by the question of whether legally to adopt his infant
son Tristram by his mistress Mavis de Vere Cole.[247] A few days
before Christmas, Tommy had a tooth extracted. Afterwards he
fell ill, and was taken by ambulance to a nursing home at Boscombe
near Bournemouth. He was said to be suffering from septicemia,
possibly as a result of a fragment of infected tooth falling into a
lung, and was also diagnosed with a rare blood condition known
as argranulocytosis, symptomatic of the abuse of cocaine. Julia was
alerted, and travelled with her father to Boscombe, where they
spent a miserable Christmas at a boarding house. Tommy wished
to see Oliver, but not Julia; he also called for his sister Helen.
He seemed to be recovering, but then developed pneumonia:
on Tuesday 5 January 1937, he died (as Bunny wrote to Mina) 'of
weakness and exhaustion'. Frances Partridge expressed the general
view that his death was attributable to the fact that 'heavy drinking
had weakened his resistance'.[248] He was two months short of his
thirty-sixth birthday (and five months short of the age at which
Lord Byron died – his fellow Harrovian, poet and bisexual seducer,
also renowned for mesmerizing looks and force of personality in
his twenties, only to disintegrate in his thirties).

Following cremation, his funeral took place on Saturday 9
January in the parish church at Ash. Apart from his relations, the

---

* This sonnet comes from a typescript of Tommy's later poems put together in the
1960s by Bunny and Julia with a view to possible publication (and now among Julia's
papers in the Berg Collection). Some of it reads rather oddly, suggesting that the
transcription (from a doubtless semi-legible manuscript) may have been faulty.

In the dark: the last picture of Tommy in Barbara's
album, probably taken in 1936

mourners (as reported in the local newspaper) included Phyllis
Keyes and H. (who jointly contributed a wreath), Frank Dobson,
Roy Harrod, and the restauranteur Rudolf Stulick.[249] The absence
of Julia, and all Tommy's Bloomsbury friends (with the exception
of Barbara Bagenal, who attended with her husband), is not to
be wondered at, for they disapproved of funerals and generally
arranged not to have them for themselves. Bunny was unable to be
there as he was suffering from influenza, but was griefstricken at
the death of the man he described in his memoirs as 'the most
brilliant and beloved of all my friends',[250] and wrote a eulogistic
appreciation for *The Times*:

There are in all circles figures universally beloved, at whose approach the faces of men and women brighten and whose departure is delayed by demonstrations from the nursery. Stephen Tomlin was one of these figures of terrific charm, with whom most ordinary people frankly fell in love, irrespective of age or sex. I shall not eulogize him as a sculptor, for though his portraits were extraordinarily full of character, and he had a craftsman's love of making things, the visual arts were necessarily inadequate to express his originality as a thinker. All criticism depends upon drawing fine distinctions. Stephen Tomlin combined the capacity of drawing important distinctions which nobody had seen before with a solid matter-of-fact common sense. From a child he had breathed in the intellectual equipment of the finest brains at the Chancery Bar, and is originality expressed itself by hair-splitting analysis of the meanings of words used in different senses, for only when double meanings are ruled out is scientific accuracy possible. His serious talk was always a delight and a surprise; full of explosive humour, yet far above taking a pleasure in a paradox for its own sake, or believing that a joke clinched an argument.

It would need the brilliance of Hazlitt's appreciations of Coleridge to describe even his superficial qualities. Much indeed of what Hazilitt says of Coleridge's intellectual wealth is directly true of Stephen Tomlin, though the natures of the two men were fundamentally dissimilar, and Stephen Tomlin never showed signs of losing his intellectual brilliance. For some years his life was overcast by profound unhappiness which was greatly augmented by the deaths, in rapid succession, of his brother Garrow and of Lytton Strachey, his wife's uncle. In a poem of this period, published anonymously, using images taken from *Alice In Wonderland*, he laid bare with extraordinary passion the pessimism which few of his generation have escaped.

> Never mind, oh never mind!
> Rest and Peace are hard to find.

But there was a certain toughness in him, physically as well as mentally, and in the last two years he was far more contented.[251] [Bunny had seen little of Tommy during those two years, and this sounds like wishful thinking.]

Virgina Woolf, in her diary for 10 January, painted a more jaundiced, but sharply-observed portrait.

> Another windless perfectly brilliant day. And Tommie [*sic*] is dead & buried yesterday, just as Clive was saying that no one had died lately... We said on the whole perhaps it was a good thing, because for the past 3 or 4 years we had scarcely seen him; when we did he seemed ravaged by his own misery; couldn't work, had been a failure; tore everyone & everything to bits in a kind of egotistic rage. Rosamond L[ehmann] said he would sit on the lawn there by the hour denouncing women, complaining of his own lot. And he had grown immensely fat, white, unwholesome looking, & was said to drink.
> Duncan said he spent most of his time in public houses near Tottenham Court Road, drinking. And Julia said no one could live with him, though she loved him. Everbody said one thing or another, as if he had cocked a snook at them & then gone off. My own intercourse with him broke over that bust, when I took a shudder at the impact of his neurotic clinging persistency, & perhaps behaved, though I didn't think so at the time, unreasonably, perversely. But he was such an egotist; such a man for confiding & getting wound up in the miserable intricacies of his own psychology. I remember his launching out on the history of his own suffering, which began, of course, with his mother & father, misunderstanding him as a child. Then there was Garrow's death, then the difficulties with Julia; how

she fell in love with someone; how he still loved her. But the odd thing was that he had, years ago, great sensibility; a human charm, & sympathy – for instance when Duncan was ill at Cassis [at Christmas 1926] – I remember how he came into the drawing room at 37 [Gordon Square] with his arms open: Nessa kissing him in tears. And then when Carrington killed herself he came round that evening to break the news so that I shouldn't get the shock first hand. Yes, I remember his curious squashed face, his suppleness, something eager & friendly & warm, quivering about him. Here he sat in the drawing room, when we lit the stove for the first time & the room was full of smoke: & he talked about me then: my work, not himself. He was extremely loquacious. Anything set him off. And he had a great gift for making people love him: Angus, Eddy, Barbara [Bagenal]. But there was something twisted, deformed in him: some shudder & profound distaste, & uneasiness. Lately he had tried, I think, living alone in the country;* didn't like it; used to haunt public houses; deserted the respectable. N[essa] & D[uncan] say they hadn't seen him for a long time. And then he catches some germ, goes into a nursing home in Boscombe, from the Johns where he was staying; the only person he wanted to see was Oliver [Strachey]: & so died aged 35. A tragic, wasted life: something wrong in it; & wrong that we shouldn't feel it more. Yet one does, in fits & starts, this very fine spring morning.

[Her brother] Adrian, who rang up, said it was a very good thing his death. That he was in a hopeless state. He had not heard of the death, only had overheard someone say 'Poor Tommie'.[252]

---

* A letter from Tommy to Bryan Guinness dated 2 November 1935 (in the family archives at Biddesden) reveals that he had just moved into a cottage in Aldington, Kent – possibly to be nearer his recently widowed mother at Upper Hardres, twelve miles distant. The other residents of the village then included Noel Coward and Ford Maddox Ford.

'No more Wheatsheaf, no more Eiffel [Tower]', noted Cyril Connolly on hearing the news, recalling the hostelries where they had caroused together.[253] And six months later, Alix Strachey wrote to Eddy Sackville-West: 'My main sorrow is about Tommy, whom I seem to miss more & more – though at the time I did not quite realise it.'[254]

Tommy photographed by Barbara in the summer of 1934

The *Puer Aeternus*: Tommy, photographed by Lytton,
off for a dip in the River Kennet

THE PUER AETERNUS

Thus ended, just half way through its biblical span, the life of Stephen 'Tommy' Tomlin – certainly a tragic life marked by unful-filled promise, and in many respects unusual and mysterious.

There is so much about it that we do not know. But what sense can we make of what we do know?

Regarding family relationships, he was always distant from, and had difficult relations with, his father. But at least until early adulthood he was close to his mother – when Bunny Garnett first saw them together in 1922, he thought that Tommy (then aged twenty-one) 'treated her as tenderly as a lover'. He was also close to the siblings nearest to him in age – his brother Garrow, three years his senior, and his sister Helen, five years his junior.

Although we know little about his own childhood, we know that, in adult life, he had great affinity with children. His nephews (sons of his older sister Joan, to whom he was not close) adored him. So did the two sons of Clive and Vanessa Bell, who longed for his visits to Charleston.

He suffered periodically from severe depression: the first instance that we know of occurred when he was just seventeen. As his brother Garrow suffered from similar episodes, there may have been a genetic tendency to depression: their mother's family, the Waterfields, possessed (according to the memoirs of one of their number[255]) a 'temperamental' strain. Obviously for much of the time Tommy was not depressed, and indeed exhibited high spirits, so one might say that he possessed a 'manic-depressive' or 'bipolar' personality – though as time passed, the 'depressive' element became increasingly pervasive.

Just as he exhibited these contrasting moods, so he also showed two contrasting patterns of behaviour in his relations with his fellow human beings. On the one hand he was engaging, life-enhancing, full of charm, able to inspire love and affection. On the other hand he possessed a brutal, malevolent, destructive streak. It was often remarked by those who knew him (including professional psychologists) that he had a 'dual personality', was a 'Jekyll and Hyde character'.

He could be wonderful company, and a brilliant conversationalist: some who knew him (and who moved in circles where they encountered many other talented people) thought him the most brilliant they had known. But his admirer Roy Harrod wrote of him: 'You might part company, grateful and pleased at having met him; there was a strong handshake, and a winning smile. You might watch him walk away with ... a suspicion of jauntiness'; but if you went after him, when he thought himself unobserved, you might catch sight of a very different figure, who found it 'hardly possibly to walk forward' and was filled with 'black and horrible despair'.[256]

In his hectic, bisexual amorous life he was constantly moving on from one lover to the next. As he never seems to have said 'no' to any sexual invitation, he certainly made some people happy; but equally he must have broken many hearts. Like Don Juan, he saw himself as a sexual conqueror, constantly employing his charm and imposing his will. The only case we know of his falling in love, wishing to concentrate all his affection on one person, is that of Henrietta Bingham – but such was both his abjectness and his possessiveness towards her that the relationship was doomed to failure. His marriage to Julia was not based on love, though they were fond of each other, he felt that life with her would provide him with inspiration and stability, and she was happy to enter into a relationship on these terms, which seems to have worked quite successfully for a couple of years.

Tonks, under whom he studied drawing, complained that he tended to leave his work unfinished; and this seems to have been a constant theme of his life – it was not just in amorous matters that he kept 'moving on'. He left Oxford after just two terms. Even his career as a sculptor he abandoned after barely a decade. Many of his sculptures (such as his bust of Barbara Bagenal) he gave up half way through; his most famous piece, the portrait head of Virginia Woolf, is incomplete. He rarely stuck at anything for very long.

At stressful moments, he tended to disappear. He performed two disappearing acts while at Oxford, causing concern to the authorities and distress to his family. At a critical moment of his life, after Henrietta had sailed for America in August 1923, none of his worried friends knew where to find him. During their marriage, Julia constantly had to put up with not knowing his whereabouts or what he was up to.

His aversion to writing letters – despite possessing considerable literary talent, and admiring 'Bloomsbury', most of whose adherents (including Julia) were dedicated correspondents – testifies to a streak of intense secretiveness. Throughout his life, he seems to have found it difficult to make or manage money, and was in constant financial difficulties. His increasing dependence on drink and drugs points to an element of self-destructive escapism.

In Jungian psychology, there is a type known as the *puer aeternus*, or boy who never grows up (named after Ovid's description of the boy-god Iacchus in his *Metamorphoses*). Such men generally have a pronounced 'mother complex'; and a feature common to many of them is 'Don Juanism', the urge to seduce numerous women. To quote Marie-Louise von Franz, the collaborator of Jung who has written what is regarded as the principal work on the *puer aeternus*:*

> The image of the mother – the image of the perfect woman who will give everything to a man and who is without any shortcomings – is sought [by the *puer aeternus*] in every woman. He is looking for a mother goddess, so that each time he is fascinated by a woman he has later to discover that she is an ordinary human being ... [and] turns away disappointed, only to project the image onto one woman after another. He eternally longs for the maternal woman who will enfold him in her arms and satisfy his every need.[257]

(Von Franz adds that a high proportion of *pueri aeterni* also tend to be homosexual – but as she believes that homosexuality is a form of mental illness, we shall not follow her notions on this subject here, except to note that Tommy managed both to be sexually interested in men and a 'Don Juan' when it came to women.) For the *puer aeternus*, just as no woman is ever quite right, so nothing in life is ever quite right – no job or vocation, for example. He therefore leads what has been described as a 'provisional life', in which he feels that whatever he is involved in at any given moment 'is *not yet* what is really wanted, and ... that some time in the future the real thing will come about'. It follows that he is eternally searching for what he cannot find, reaching for what he cannot grasp. Von Franz continues:

> This attitude ... means a constant refusal to commit oneself to the moment... The one situation dreaded by such a man is to be bound to anything whatsoever. There is a terrific fear of being

* With apologies for the imperfect English of either Von Franz or her translator, it is not clear which.

pinned down... There is always the fear of being caught in a situation from which it may be impossible to slip out again.[258]

As the name suggests, the *puer aeternus* (like Peter Pan) remains psychologically frozen in adolescence. This produces various consequences. When it comes to work,

> the *puer aeternus* can work ... when fascinated or in a state of great enthusiasm. Then he can work twenty-four hours at a stretch or even longer... But what he cannot do is to work on a dreary, rainy morning when work is boring and one has to kick oneself into it; that is the one thing the *puer aeternus* cannot manage and will use any kind of excuse to avoid.[259]

As *pueri aeterni* are usually incapable of steady work, they often have problems with money, and sometimes resort to obtaining it in irregular ways.[260] On the other hand, what they lack in application they make up for in charm.

> Many have the charm of youth and the stirring [*sic*] quality of a glass of champagne. *Pueri aeterni* are generally very agreeable to talk with: they usually have interesting subjects to talk about and have an invigorating effect upon the listener; they do not like conventional situations; they ask deep questions and go straight for the truth... Usually the youthful charm of the *puer aeternus* is prolonged through later stages of life.[261]

However, the charm often masks a brutal side: this is the inevitable consequence of moving on from one woman to the next, for 'cold brutality comes out every time he leaves the woman. When his feeling has gone, out comes an ice-cold brutality with no human feeling in it, and the whole sentimental enthusiasm is projected onto another woman.'[262]

Obviously these are rough-and-ready generalisations regarding the tendencies of a particular human type. But it is hardly necessary to draw the parallels with Tommy – who was attached to his mother; who seduced one person after another; who was constantly moving on, refusing to be pinned down to any person or project; who (so far as we know) only once believed he had found the ideal mate he sought (whereupon he behaved in a way likely to alienate her); who was a brilliant talker; who could display great charm and equally great brutality; who was always in financial difficulties; and who (we are told) exhibited great grief at the drowning of a youth said to be the model for Peter Pan.

Von Franz also tells us that the *puer aeternus* often shows 'a fascination for dangerous sports, particularly flying and mountaineering, so as to get as high as possible, the symbolism of which is to get away from the mother – i.e. from the earth, from ordinary life', and that 'many such men die at a young age in airplane crashes and mountaineering accidents'.[263] This might certainly be taken to apply to Tommy's brother Garrow, who died in an air crash – he too was clearly a 'Don Juan' and a *puer aeternus*. In Tommy's case, the desire 'to get as high as possible' so as to escape 'from ordinary life' manifested itself in his addiction to drugs and alcohol, which led just as surely to an early death.

Von Franz takes as a typical example of the *puer aeternus* the French writer and aviator Antoine de Saint-Exupéry (1900–44), who is presumed to have died in an air crash (the wreckage was never found). Though they led very different lives (and are unlikely to have met), Saint-Exupéry had much in common with his contemporary Tommy (to whom he bore a passing physical resemblence). Having been close to his mother, he became a great charmer and heartbreaker. He suffered greatly from the (non-combattant) death of a brother in 1917. He took opium. He was given to bad moods and fits of rage. He contracted a marriage which became unhappy: his wife remembered him 'walking up and down from morning to evening' in a depressed state. He wrote few letters. He preferred the company of children to adults, beginning his best-known work, *Le Petit Prince*, with the reflection: 'I have lived a great deal among grown-ups. I have seen them intimately, close at hand. And that hasn't much improved my opinion of them… So I lived my life alone, without anyone that I could really talk to.' He was constantly in search of (but never found) some kind of religious meaning to life. He possessed what Von Franz describes as 'a nostalgic longing for death'.[264] As he was so elusive, and left so few traces of his doings, he has proved a problem for his biographers. So it is with Tommy.

Now weather-beaten and lichen-covered, its lettering barely decipherable, this stone in the churchyard at Ash bears the names and dates of Lord and Lady Tomlin and their three sons. The eldest son was buried in New Zealand, where he died; the others were cremated following funerals at Ash, and their ashes (including Tommy's) presumably lie beneath the stone, placed after Lady Tomlin's death in 1948.

I

Hear thou, and digest my answer,
   O corrupter of my youth,
(Couched in this thy chosen stanza,)
   — Whence thy smug contempt of Truth?

II

Elegant thy panegyric,
   Yet thou touchest not my heart,
Yet I can but count thy lyric
   Prostitution of Fine Art.

III

Though thou sung my forebears praises
   With inspired minstrelsy,
And enumerate their phases
   Of incipient lunacy,

APPENDIX I

[To Leo Myers, 1919; written on paper headed by Harrow School crest. MS in Eton College Archives.]

I

Hear thou, and digest my answer,
O corrupter of my youth,
(Couched in this thy chosen stanza,)
– Whence thy smug contempt of truth?

II

Elegant thy panegyric,
Yet thou touchest not my heart,
Yet I cannot count thy lyric
Prostitution of thine Art.

III

Though thou sing my forebears' praises
With inspiréd minstrelsy
And ennumerate their phases
Of incipient Lunacy,

IV

Thou dost wish (and well I know it)
Weaned of the Castalian* spring
Me, an unexpected poet,
Hectic rhapsodies to sing.

V

At that spring I'll hold my dwelling,
Though the river flows afar;
At the spring a song's more telling
Than a moaning at the bar!†

VI

For 'tis there that they would send me
(Pray excuse the metaphor:
Play of words on 'bar' will end me
In intricacies galore!)

VII

Well I ween (though thou deny it),
Fain this moral thou wouldst tell,
'Not, not the bar! – for if thou try it,
Truly thou shall find it Hell.'

---

* A spring near Delphi, thought by the Romans to be a source of poetic inspiration.
† An allusion to the first stanza of Tennyson's poem *Crossing the Bar*:

Sunset and evening star,
And one clear call for me!
And may there be no moaning of the bar,
When I put out to sea.

VIII

Such I deem would be thy counsel
Shouldst thou speak from jest apart.
(Some would call it sowing groundsel
Mid the good grain of thy heart.)

IX

Yet despite thy true opinion,
Thou hast furnished ample proof
That my soul is but a minion
Cringing at a stern reproof!

APPENDIX II

To H[elen] R[osa] T[omlin]

[On graduating from Oxford in 1928, Tommy's sister Helen spurned her parents's suggestion that she should become a companion to her mother at Clifton Place, and enrolled for a Diploma in Anthropology at London University]

O Helen dear, you really oughter
Be more your mother's model daughter.
(For instance, you're a dreadful sinner
In often being late for dinner.)
Why must you smoke and quaff your beer?
Why must you hunt for a career?
Why can't you take an active share
In Charity or After-Care
Or, as befits exalted rank,
Officiate in the Penny Bank?
Why can't you show some piety
Like most girls in Society?
You'd find a month of Early Church
Would make you happier than Research.
You should employ your leisure hours
Among your books, among your flowers:
Cutting away at frocks and capes
Instead of Prehistoric Apes.
Why must you read of Tribal Marriage
Instead of riding in a carriage?
Your endless Academic toils

Will only culminate in boils.
Up then, and strive to act with grace
At Angley Park and Clifton Place,*
A cheerful, willing, gentle girl,
Not a mere intellectual churl.
And be to all th'example good
Of modest English womanhood.

[1929]

* The country and London residences of the Tomlin family.

APPENDIX III

THE SLUGGARD'S QUADRILLE
By The Lobster

[This poem, originally published in the *New Statesman and Nation* on 20 May 1933, is packed with literary allusions. Where it has been possible to identify these, footnotes are given. No doubt some identifications have eluded the present authors.]

I

At Evening, the devouring Tide
Of Night will wash me from your side.
I talk, and read, and play, and drink,
One eye upon the distant brink,
One eye upon the Dorsal Fin
That circles, ever closer in.
The Shark is greedy, strong and wise
(The only fish that blinks its eyes).
It's mouth with rows and rows of teeth
Is situated underneath.
But how avert, and how delay
The drowning of this Concrete Day?
The noble hills and landmarks dear
Are islanded, and disappear.
The water's dark and glistening lips
Nuzzle the steeples at their tips,

And far below, as thought in wells,
I hear these Mournful Evening Bells.*

The air is dark, the sea is dark,
Pressed close, and heaving, face to face
Like lovers in a secret place,
Like lovers in a gloomy park;
And someone passing near at hand
Hears murmuring sounds and words he cannot
     understand.

My darling books are grappling hooks
To clutch the fast receding shore.
And still I toil with midnight oil†
To calm the gathering water's roar.
In vain! In vain!
Comes silent, flooding in, the main.‡
The anchor drags and Ah, my heart!
The trusted cables strain and part!

Alone, alone! I float alone!
The crazy timbers of my bed
Bear up with many a croak and groan
The uneasy weight of flesh and bone
And echoing box that is my head.

---

* 'The soft, distant, mournful evening bell,/ So full of music and melodious sounds...' John Walker Ord, *Written on Arthur's Seat.*
† 'Whence is thy learning? Hath thy toil/ O'er books consumed the midnight oil?' John Gay, *Shepherd and Philosopher.*
‡ 'Far back through creeks and inlets making/ Comes silent, flooding in, the main.' Arthur Hugh Clough, *Say Not, the Struggle Naught Availeth.*

Never an oar, and never a compass,
Ambushed round by Shark and Grampus,
Without sail, without a helm,
Riding with short uneasy motion,*
Soon the waves must overwhelm
This matchbox on a tainted ocean!
White horses arch their ribbèd necks,
And shake their manes across their decks.
Their baleful eyes the seas illume
All marbled with the drifting spume.
The vast reticulated skin
Breaks, and the ocean lets me in.
Ah! She founders by the prow!
Pity the wet sea-boy† now!

Suspended in the glassy sea
The Shark is nosing up to me,
Hanging there like fruit in jelly.
He wallows over, shows his belly.
Shows his dreadful dreaming mouth.
How wonderful God's works appear,
Poor Jonah, when you see them near!
Ah, swallow, swallow, flying south!‡
I'm frozen to stone by this head of a Gorgon!
He's swallowed the fig that goes on the thistle!§

* 'The Sun, right up above the mast,/ Had fix'd her to the ocean:/ But in a minute she 'gan stir,/ With a short uneasy motion – /Backwards and forwards half her length/ With a short uneasy motion.' Samuel Taylor Coleridge, *The Rime of the Ancient Mariner*.
† 'Canst thou, O partial sleep, give thy repose/ To the wet sea-boy in an hour so rude,/ And in the calmest and most stillest night,/ With all appliances and means to boot,/ Deny it to a king?' Shakespeare, *King Henry IV, Part Two*, Act III, Scene 1.
‡ 'O Swallow, Swallow, flying, flying South…' Tennyson, *The Princess*.
§ 'Do men gather grapes of thorns, or figs of thistles?' *St Matthew*, 7:16.

He's taken the pea right out of the whistle!
He's carried away the main pipe of the Organ.
But what does it matter? Oh what does it matter?
Life without music is safer, though flatter.

Down through the clear entrails of the sea compressing,
     dilating,
Slowly, softly revolving; with a taut and delicate thrill
Slipping from side to side; perpendicular rollar-skating,
Out of the noise of the storm and the tide, where the
     waters are fixed and still.

So falls a leaf that is dead,
Or the wingèd sycamore seed,
On a quiet autumn day,
With a motion gentle and gay
Fulfilling a gloomy need.
And the starlings wheel overhead.

There at last the body lies,
Feels the solid silver sands
Trickle through its sleeping hands,
Lies at last where it would wish.
And in the green translucent skies
Wheel the voiceless tribe of fish.

But though full fathom five it lies,
No pearls are gendered in its eyes,*
But oyster-like gummed sill to sill,
When they wake, they're oysters still.

---

* 'Full fathom five thy father lies./ Of his bones are coral made,/ Those are pearls that were his eyes:/ Nothing of him that doth fade.' Shakespeare, *The Tempest*, Act I Scene 2.

Nothing rich and nothing strange
As coral breeds of this sea-change.
But in the joints, inert and placid,
Form crystals of the Uric Acid.

Then in the garden of my dreams,
Where the dark Panther growls and rumbles,
The Knife is waved, the Pie-crust crumbles,
Athene's Bird protests and screams.
I am the Owl. I am the Pie.
The spoon, the dish, the Panther – I.*
And ere dawn whitens in the East
I celebrate the dismal feast.

Never mind, oh never mind!
Rest and Peace are hard to find.

II

Too soon, all too soon
Slides down the watery moon,
Draws from field and house and hedge
The Night-tide over the world's edge.
How salt, estranging, and how drear
The emerging shoals of Day appear!

* This stanza alludes to verse recited by Alice in Chapter X of her *Adventures in Wonderland.*

I passed by his garden and marked with one eye,
How the Owl and the Panther were sharing a pie.
The Panther took pie-crust and gravy and meat,
While the Owl had the dish as his share of the treat.
When the pie was all finished the Owl, as a boon,
Was kindly permitted to pocket the spoon.

Though here the waters still lie deep,
I hear the breakers in my sleep,
And feel the approaching shore.
The ceiling lowers with every billow,
And soon will break upon my pillow,
And I shall sleep no more.
The Land that loved me, now would kill.
Ah, leave me, leave me, sleeping still!

Still ebbs the tide, and round my face
The surf begins to break and boil,
And lifts me from my quiet place,
And shakes me in its harsh turmoil,
And flings me on remorseless rocks,
And tears me, stifles me, and knocks
My senseless body, skin and bones
Like bags of walnuts on the stones.
At last it throws beyond its reach,
And leaves me stranded on the beach.

Half dead like Gulliver I lie
And little Hates, with cords and pegs
And Lilliputtian despairs,
Puncture my skin and pull my hairs,
Tie down my nerveless arms and legs
Beneath unanswering alien sky.

And when at last I turn my head,
What dreary flotsam round me spread!
What sponges, bladder-wrack, and shells!
What gloomy snakes! What fishy smells!
What brushes, towels, studs and pins!
What combs and razors, tubes and tins,

And little bottles from the sea
That hold no messages from me!

Too brown, upon the drying sand
The daylight bakes me far too brown.*
I leave my bed and turn inland,
Where rocks and precipices frown,
To seek the meadow and the town.

I rise with pain and leave my bed
To wash and curl my monstrous head
And hang it in despair.
No sugar that the grocer stocks
Brings back the hyacinth to my locks,
Or gilds this greying hair!
I strive with nerves and senses dim
My buttons and my belt to trim,
And set my shoulders square.
The Pobble can no more regain
Position One, though toes remain.

But when at length the desert yields
To the enamelled noon-day fields,
And all around the hills display
In the dear light of common day†
Village and meadow, stream and town,
Sweet interspace of grove and down,
And sounds and smells, a loving train,
Crowd in to comfort me again,

* 'Tis the voice of the Lobster; I heard him declare, / "You have baked me too
brown, I must sugar my hair." *Alice's Adventures in Wonderland*, Chapter X.
† 'At length the Man perceives it die away,/ And fade into the light of common day.'
Wordsworth, *Intimations of Immortality from Recollections of Early Childhood*.

Then to my heart a hope returns,
And once again the spirit burns!
I hail my friends across the street.
I feel the wings upon my feet,
And there, beneath the soaring larks,
I speak contemptuously of Sharks.

It is a dreadful thing for me
To find myself each night – at Sea.

Ah, Land! Dear Land, inconstant Land!
Have I not fed you with my tears?
Did I not, in my childish years,
Salute you with my royal hand?
Did I not love your Cakes and Ales?*
Have I not praised your Nightingales?

III

The Dead shall rise again, they say.
They say the sea gives up its dead.†
Upon the ninth or seventh day
The Drowned stir in the oozy bed
And, like a guest that goes away
On sudden whim with nothing said,‡
Glide to the surface overhead.

* 'Dost thou think that, because thou art virtuous, there shall be no more cakes and ale?' Shakespeare, *Twelfth Night*, Act II, Scene 3.
† 'And the sea gave up the dead which were in it; and death and hell delivered up the dead which were in them: and they were judged every man according to their works.' *Revelation* 20:13.
‡ The Bloomsberries were notorious for leaving social gatherings without saying goodbye.

The sea is stretched inert as lead
In the chill early morning air.
On its astonished face they spread
And burst, like lilies, there.

'Will you walk a little straighter?' said a clergyman I knew,
'There's a Porpoise in our life here, and a Task for me and you.
'You can really have no notion how delightful it will be
'When they hake us up and stand us all around the Glassy Sea!'
But I replied 'Too far! Too far!' and gave a look askance –
Could not, would not, could not, would not, could not join
       the dance.

'What matters it how far we go?'
A Scaly Friend replied,
'So long as we can surely know
'There is no other side?'

*   These two stanzas are closely based on the following song sung by the Mock
Turtle in Chapter X of *Alice's Adventures in Wonderland*:

'Will you walk a little faster?' said a whiting to a snail.
'There's a porpoise close behind us and he's treading on my tail.
See how eagerly the lobster and the turtles all advance!
They are waiting on the shingle – will you come and join the dance?

Will you, won't you, will you, won't you, will you join the dance?
Will you won't you, will you, won't you, won't you join the dance?

'You can really have no notion how delightful it will be
When they take us up and throw us, with the lobsters, out to sea!'

But the snail replied 'Too far, too far!' and gave a look askance –
Said he thanked the whiting kindly, but he would not join the dance.

Would not, could not, would not, could not, would not join the dance.
Would not, could not, would not, could not, could not join the dance.

'What matters it how far we go?' his scaly friend replied.
'There is another shore, you know, upon the other side.
The further off from England the nearer is to France –
Then turn not pale, beloved snail, but come and join the dance…'

Though suitorless, the careful web
I weave by day, by night's undone.
Ah, for that Flood that knows no ebb,
Whose western rim shall quench the sun!
Sunset, and Evening star,
And one clear call for me –
'Time, Gentlemen!' – across the bar,
And I'll put out to Sea,*
And will encounter, pleased and brave,
The tideless ocean of the grave,
Where Ark can find no Ararat† –
Content, if I am sure of that.
Where shafts of dawn no more will prise
The unwilling shutters of the eyes,
Nor find the body, gashed and splay,
Stranded upon the reefs of Day.

---

* See final footnote to Appendix I.
† The mountain, now in eastern Turkey, where, according to *Genesis* 8:4, Noah's Ark came to rest after the great flood.

NOTES

'ST'=Stephen Tomlin; 'Berg' = Berg Collection, New York Public Library; 'BL' = British Library; 'King's' = Archives of King's College, Cambridge; 'Tate' = Tate Gallery Archives; 'UCL' = Julia Strachey Collection, University College, London

1 Information about genealogy of Baron Tomlin in *The Complete Peerage* and *Burke's Peerage*; information from Philip Trower.

2 Anne Oliver Bell (ed.), *The Diary of Virginia Woolf*, Vol. V (1984), pp. 47–8.

3 Information from Philip Trower.

4 Information from Philip Trower.

5 Memoir by ST's sister, Helen Goldby, of her Tomlin grandmother and her 'Boots' (made available by her daughter Libby Goldby).

6 See especially *The Dog at Clambercrown* (1955).

7 John Joliffe (ed.), *Raymond Asquith: Life and Letters* (1980), p. 50.

8 Information provided by the Harrow School archivist, Ms J. K. Badrock, and gleaned from *The Harrovian*, 1914–17.

9 Copy of ST's prize poem *Jerusalem* (including explanatory note) in possession of his niece Libby Goldby.

10 See Claire Harman, *Sylvia Townsend Warner: A Biography* (London, 1989), Ch.1.

11 Sylvia Townsend Warner, 'Out of my Happy Past', in *New Yorker*, 9 August 1941 (also included in her collection *A Garland of Straw* [1943]): this ostensible short story is clearly a memoir relating to Tommy, who appears under the name of Billy Williams.

12 Muriel Box, *Rebel Advocate: A Life of Gerald Gardiner* (London, 1983), pp. 15–16; Judith M. Heimann, *The Most Offending Soul Alive* (1997), pp. 13–14.

13 *The Harrovian*, 27 July 1917, 19 October 1918.

14 Passenger List of RMS Remuera sailing from Plymouth to New Zealand, 29 March 1916 (see numbers 18–19): http://www.oocities.org/heartland/estates/8053/remuera.html. Call-up list of Christchurch and Canterbury men, 2 October 1917 (see North Canterbury section): https://paperspast.natlib.govt.nz/newspapers/SUNCH19171002.2.92.2. Notice of Anthony Tomlin's death in Timaru Herald: https://paperspast.natlib.govt.nz/newspapers/THD19171207.2.14. Anthony Tomlin's grave in Timaru cemetery: https://billiongraves.com/grave/Anthony-Neville-Chesshyre-Tomlin/14637457#/.

15 MS in possession of Libby Goldby.

16 Warner, op. cit.

17 Ibid.

18 Information provided by New College archivist Jennifer Thorp, notably from manuscript volume minuting meetings of the Warden and Tutors, 1902–1922.

19 C. M. Bowra, *Memories: 1898–1939* (1966), p. 116.

20 BL Add MSS 71190, 71194, 71616, 72762, 72763.

21 Roy Harrod to Julia Tomlin, 17 January
    1937, in Julia Strachey papers (UCL).

22 R. F. Harrod, *The Life of John Maynard
    Keynes* (London, 1951), pp. 189–91.

23 R. F. Harrod, *The Prof: A Personal Memoir
    of Lord Cherwell* (1959), pp. 114–16.

24 Harrod, *The Life of John Maynard Keynes*,
    loc. cit.

25 BL Add MSS 72767, f. 145.

26 ST to Henrietta Bingham, 2 September
    1923 in Henrietta Worth Bingham
    Papers, Sophia Smith Collection, Smith
    College.

27 Gerald Brenan, *Personal Record* (1975),
    p. 155.

28 Letter-poem from Stephen Tomlin to
    Leo Myers in Eton College Archives,
    MS 447.01 (undated, but written on
    paper headed with crest of Harrow
    School).

29 Harman, pp. 44–5.

30 Ibid., p. 47.

31 Ibid., p. 68.

32 Houghton Library, Harvard; quoted by
    Neville Jason in *The Sculpture of Frank
    Dobson* (Henry Moore Foundation, 1994),
    p. 38, and by Oliver Garnett in *The
    Sculpture of Stephen Tomlin* (Cambridge
    University BA Dissertation, 1979; copy
    in Tate Gallery Archives).

33 Frank Dobson autobiography in
    Henry Moore Institute, Leeds.

34 *The Sculpture of Frank Dobson*, p. 43,
    based on information provided by
    Sylvia Gilley, an assistant to Dobson in
    the 1930s.

35 Information from Philip Trower.

36 Harman, pp. 47–8.

37 Judith Stinton, *Chaldon Herring: The
    Powys Circle in a Dorset Village* (Boydell
    Press, 1988), p. 69.

38 David Garnett (ed.), *Dora Carrington:
    Letters* (London, 1970), p. 339.

39 Sylvia Townsend Warner, 'Theodore
    Powys and Some Friends at East
    Chaldon, 1922–1927: A Narrative and
    Some Letters' in *The Powys Review*,
    No. 5, Summer 1979 [*TPSF*].

40 Quoted in http://www.hermitary.com/
    bookreviews/powys-tf.html.

41 Malcolm Elwyn (ed.), *Letters of John
    Cowper Powys to his Brother Llewellyn*,
    Vol. I (London, 1975), p. 294.

42 *TPSF*.

43 *TPSF*; Harman, *Sylvia Townsend Warner*,
    pp. 48–50.

44 David Garnett, *The Familiar Faces* (1962),
    pp. 1–2.

45 Richard Garnett (ed.), *Sylvia & David*
    (1994), p. 35.

46 *TPSF*.

47 *Sylvia & David*, p. 35.

48 Quoted in Richard Garnett, 'Theodore
    Powys and the Garnetts: Records of a
    Friendship' in *The Powys Journal*, Volume
    XI (2001) [*TPG*], pp. 9–10.

49 ST to David Garnett, undated, in
    Garnett Papers, Northwestern
    University; also quoted in *TPG*, p. 10.

50 *The Familiar Faces*, pp. 3–6.

51 *Sylvia & David*, p. 35.

52 ST to David Garnett, Garnett Papers,
    Northwestern University.

53 Quoted in Sarah Knights, *Bloomsbury's
    Outsider: A Life of David Garnett* (2015),
    p. 175.

54 The campaign to get Theo's work
    published described in some detail by
    Richard Garnett in *TPG*.

55 ST to Roy Harrod, November 1923;
    BL Add MSS 72763 ff. 73-4.

56 Quoted in Stinton, p. 53.

57 Quoted in Stinton, p. 70.

58 See ST to David Garnett, 1 November
    1923, in Garnett Papers, Northwestern
    University (quoted in *TPG*, p. 17); Sylvia

Townsend Warner, 'Theodore Powys at East Chaldon', in Belinda Humfrey (ed.) *Recollections of the Powys Brothers* (1980), pp. 128–30.

59 *TPG.*

60 David Garnett, *The Familiar Faces*, pp. 12–13.

61 *Ibid.*, pp. 2-3; Knights, *Bloomsbury's Outsider*.

62 Gerald Brenan, *Personal Record*, pp. 154–5.

63 Quoted in Frances Spalding, *Duncan Grant* (1997), p. 253.

64 Duncan Grant to Vanessa Bell in Tate Gallery Archives, 24 April 1923.

65 David Garnett, pp. 9, 11–12.

66 Emily Bingham, *Irrepressible: The Jazz Age Life of Henrietta Bingham* (Farrar, Straus & Giroux, New York, 2015), pp. 93–145, *passim*.

67 ST to Henrietta Bingham, 27 August 1923 (quoted in Bingham).

68 Ibid., 13 April 1923.

69 Ibid., 7 April 1923.

70 Ibid., 24 May 1923.

71 Ibid., 26 March 1923, 27 August 1923, 2 September 1923.

72 David Garnett, pp. 14–15.

73 David Garnett to Mina Kirstein, 10 August 1923 (Berg).

74 ST to Henrietta Bingham, 27 August 1923 (quoted in Bingham, p. 105).

75 David Garnett to Mina Kirstein, 14 September 1923 (Berg).

76 Ibid., 6 September 1923.

77 Marion Tomlin to Henrietta Bingham, 30 July 1923, in Bingham Papers.

78 Letter of October 1923 in Bingham Papers.

79 Ibid., 9 October 1923.

80 David Garnett, p. 117.

81 Robert Medley, *Drawn from Life* (1983), p. 62.

82 BL Add MSS 72763 ff. 73–4.

83 Bingham, pp. 108–10.

84 Bingham, pp. 112–14.

85 David Garnett, pp. 61–2; David Garnett to Mina Kirstein, March 1924, Berg.

86 Bingham, pp. 114–15.

87 Quoted in Bingham, p. 89.

88 Lincoln Kirstein, *Mosaic Memoirs* (1994), pp. 63–4.

89 Quoted in Bingham, p. 119.

90 ST to Henrietta Bingham, 13 August 1924 (quoted in Bingham, p. 128).

91 Bingham, Ch. 8.

92 ST to Dora Carrington, undated (BL).

93 Percy Meisel and Walter Kendrick, *Bloomsbury-Freud: The Letters of James and Alix Strachey, 1924–5* (1986), p. 136.

94 David Garnett, pp. 36-8.

95 Membership lists of Cranium Club in papers of David Garnett, Roy Harrod, Sebastian Sprott.

96 Quoted in Bingham, p. 135.

97 Bingham, p. 138.

98 Quoted in Bingham, p. 136.

99 Quoted in Bingham, p. 139.

100 Gerald Brenan to Dora Carrington, 18 May 1925 (quoted in Bingham, p. 145).

101 Tommy to J. M. Keynes, March 1925, in Keynes Papers, British Library.

102 Anne Olivier Bell (ed.), *The Diary of Virginia Woolf*, Vol.II (1978), entry for 21 December 1924.

103 Virginia Woolf to Jaques Raverat, 5 February 1925, in Nigel Nicolson (ed.), *The Letters of Virginia Woolf*, Vol.III (1977), p. 164.

104 Lytton Strachey papers, British Library.

105 Frances Partridge, *Memories* (1981), p. 139.

106 Gerald Brenan, *Personal Record*, pp. 154–5.

107 Knights, pp. 220–4.

108 Frances Spalding, *Duncan Grant*, p. 272.

109 Quentin Bell in *Charleston Past and Present* (1987).

110 Quoted in Michael Holroyd, *Lytton Strachey*, Vol. II (1968), p. 527.

111 See Richard Keynes (ed.), *Lydia and Maynard: The Letters of Lydia Lopokova and John Maynard Keynes* (1992), letter of 28 May 1923.

112 Michael Holroyd, *Lytton Strachey* (1994), pp. 547-51. (Holroyd incorrectly states that Ralph played the Executioner – a copy of the programme in the Theatre Museum shows it was in fact Tommy.)

113 Richard Garnett (ed.), *Sylvia and David: The Townsend Warner/Garnett Letters* (1994), entry for 15 October 1967.

114 David Garnett, pp. 64-5; Partridge, p. 92.

115 See Michael De-la-Noy, *Eddy: The Life of Edward Sackville-West* (1988).

116 Vanessa to Duncan (Tate).

117 Quoted in De-la-Noy, p. 107.

118 Vanessa Bell to Virginia Woolf, 7 January 1926, in Nicolson (ed.), *The Letters of Virginia Woolf*, Vol.III, p.226.

119 Ibid., p.227 (Virginia to Vanessa, 9 January 1926).

120 De-la-Noy, pp. 129-30.

121 Undated letter from Banting in David Garnett Papers, Northwestern University.

122 De-la-Noy, pp. 130-1.

123 Ibid, p. 107.

124 ST to Julia, June 1927, in Julia Strachey Papers, UCL. Tommy writes that he was dining with Bunny in a restaurant and criticising Sylvia when she herself walked in, to their embarrassment. 'However, she was pleasant and it passed off well enough. I think she did not hear our slanders.'

125 Harman, *Sylvia Townsend Warner*, p. 68.

126 Dora Carrington to Lytton Strachey, 4 June 1926 (BL).

127 Dora Carrington to Gerald Brenan, 10 July 1926.

128 Lytton Strachey to Roger Senhouse, 9 August 1926 (Berg).

129 Brenan, p. 172.

130 Holroyd (1968), p. 569.

131 Ibid., p.575.

132 Tommy to Julia, September 1926, in Julia Strachey papers, UCL.

133 The letters from Julia to Carrington, 1926–32, are held in the Berg Collection

134 Vanessa Bell to Duncan Grant, 7 January 1927 (Tate).

135 Virginia Woolf to Vanessa Bell, from Sicily, 14 April 1927, in *The Letters of Virginia Woolf*, Vol. III, p. 363.

136 Vanessa Bell to Virginia Woolf, 23 April 1927 (Berg).

137 Undated letter from ST to Roy Harrod in Harrod papers, BL.

138 Lytton Strachey papers, BL.

139 Kathleen Hale, *A Slender Reputation* (1994), p. 132.

140 Incomplete and undated letter from Tommy to Julia in Julia Strachey papers, UCL, probably written in late June 1927 as it refers to a solar eclipse which took place then.

141 Partridge, *Memories*, pp. 112-17. (Frances says the day in question was in May; but Lytton refers to the party having just taken place in a letter dated 22 June.)

142 Julia Strachey and Frances Partridge, *Julia* (1983), p. 107.

143 Ibid., p. 108.

144 Lincoln Kirstein, *Mosaic Memoirs*, p.64.

145 Quoted in Holroyd (1968), pp. 585-6.

146 Nicolson (ed.), *The Letters of Virginia Woolf*, Vol. III (Chatto & Windus, 1977), p. 401, quoted by kind permission of Random House Group Ltd.

147 Information from Philip Trower.

148 Carrington to Lytton, September 1927 (BL); *Julia*, pp. 108-9.

149 Information from Duncan Speight, Librarian of Lincoln's Inn.

150 Quoted in Oliver Garnett, *The Sculpture of Stephen Tomlin*, p. 29.

151 Ibid., p. 28.

152 Lytton to Dadie Rylands (King's).

153 Information from Francis Ford.

154 Holroyd (1994 edition), p. 627.

155 Julia to Carrington, undated (probably 1930) (Berg).

156 David Pryce-Jones (ed.), *Cyril Connolly: Journal and Memoir* (New York, 1984), p. 201.

157 Diaries of Edith Olivier in Wiltshire Record Office, Chippenham.

158 *Julia*, p. III.

159 Cecil Beaton and Richard Buckle (ed.), *Self-Portrait with Friends: The Selected Diaries of Cecil Beaton*, 6 April 1930; Edith Olivier, *From her Journals, 1924–48* (1989), 6 April 1930.

160 Augustus John, *Chiaroscuro* (1952), p. 90.

161 Julia to Carrington, 4 February 1929 (Berg); *Julia*, p. III.

162 *Julia*, pp. 112-3.

163 Carrington papers (BL).

164 Information from Philip Trower.

165 Valentine Ackland, *For Sylvia: An Honest Account* (1985), p. 125.

166 *Julia*, Chapter II.

167 Pryce-Jones (ed.), *Cyril Connolly: Journal and Memoir*, p. 244 (April 1934).

168 *Julia*, pp. 127-30.

169 Sackville-West papers (BL).

170 Dora Carrington to Julia Strachey (BL).

171 Vanessa Bell to Duncan Grant, February 1930 (Tate).

172 Julia Strachey to Dora Carrington, February 1930 (Berg).

173 Edith's diary (Chippenham), 12 July 1930.

174 *Julia*, p.114.

175 Lytton-Carrington correspondence (BL).

176 ST to Julian Bell, 17 October 1930 (King's).

177 Virginia Woolf to Vanessa Bell, 2 November 1930 (Berg).

178 Dora Carrington to Sebastian Sprott, 7 October 1930 (King's); Oliver Garnett, op. cit.

179 Frances Partridge, *Good Company* (1994), entry for 7 May 1967.

180 Diana Mosley, *A Life of Contrasts* (1977), chapter 8.

181 Dorothy Bussy to André Gide, 22 December 1924, quoted in *Selected Letters of André Gide and Dorothy Bussy*.

182 Julia Strachey to Dora Carrington (inaccurately dated February 1932) (Berg).

183 *Julia*, pp. 114-17.

184 Oliver Garnett, *The Sculpture of Stephen Tomlin*, pp. 36-8.

185 Quentin Bell, *Virginia Woolf: A Biography*, Vol. II (1972), p. 160.

186 Virginia Woolf to Dorothy Bussy, 22 July 1931, in Nigel Nicolson (ed.), *The Letters of Virginia Woolf*, Vol. IV (1978), p.360.

187 Ibid.

188 Anne Oliver Bell (ed.), *The Diary of Virginia Woolf*, Vol. V (1984), pp. 47-8.

189 Quentin Bell, p. 261.

190 Oliver Garnett, pp. 40-1.

191 James Gardiner, *A Class Apart: The Private Pictures of Montague Glover* (1992).

192 Undated letters of Dora Carrington in papers of Sebastian Sprott (King's).

193 Lytton Strachey to Roger Senhouse, 3 April and 7 April 1927 (Berg).

194 David Garnett, *The Familiar Faces*, pp. 118–9.

195 Dame Alix Meynell, *Public Servant, Private Woman: An Autobiography* (1988), pp. 74-7, 95-6, 103-4, 108-25.

196 David Garnett, pp. 120-6.

197 Anne Olivier Bell (ed.), *The Diary of Virginia Woolf*, Vol. IV (1982), entry for 1 January 1932.

198 Brenan, *Personal Record*, pp. 242–4.

199 Carrington's journal (BL).

200 Ibid., p. 66.

201 Quoted in Holroyd (1994), p. 684.

202 Julia Strachey to Ralph Partridge (King's).

203 Brenan, p. 246.

204 Holroyd, p. 694.

205 Rosamond Lehmann to Dadie Rylands, undated but referring to imminent appearance of her new novel which was published May 1932 (King's).

206 Oliver Garnett, *The Sculpture of Stephen Tomlin*, p. 42.

207 Frances Spalding, *Duncan Grant*, p. 323.

208 David Garnett to Mina Curtiss, 2 February 1937 (Berg).

209 Oliver Garnett, p. 44.

210 Copy of undated letter from Julia Strachey to ST in David Garnett's papers, Northwestern University.

211 Anne Chisholm, *Frances Partridge*, p. 156.

212 *Julia*, p. 14.

213 Ibid., p. 108.

214 David Garnett, *The Familiar Faces*, p. 151.

215 See letter on this subject from Virginia to Angus Davidson, 11 April 1935, in *The Letters of Virginia Woolf*.

216 Frances Partridge to Rosamond Lehmann, 22 February 1981 (King's).

217 Quoted in Selina Hastings, *Rosamond Lehmann* (2002), p. 151.

218 Frances Partridge, *Good Company*, entry for 7 May 1967,

219 Frances Partridge to Rosamond Lehmann, 30 May 1983 (King's).

220 Rosamond Lehmann to James Lees-Milne, 6 September 1983 (JLM Papers, Beinecke Library, Yale).

221 Rosamond Lehmann to Dadie Rylands, 30 November 1932 (King's).

222 Bryan Guinness to Roy Harrod, 16 October 1932, in BL/Add MS 71183.

223 Diaries of Julia Strachey, and letters to her from Wogan Philipps (Berg).

224 *Julia*, pp. 122–3.

225 Undated letter from Wogan Philipps to Julia Strachey (Berg).

226 Tommy's abusive behaviour towards Julia is graphically referred to in several of the love letters to her (mostly undated) from Wogan (Berg).

227 *Julia*, p. 136.

228 *Julia*, p. 124.

229 Hopkins, Kenneth (ed.), *The Letters of Gamel Woolsey to Llewelyn Powys 1930–1939* (1983).

230 Julia Strachey to Frances Partridge, 25 March 1935 (King's).

231 Wogan Philipps to Barbara Ker-Seymer, 30 August 1934, in Ker-Seymer Papers (Tate).

232 Copy of letter from H. to Tommy, dated 'Wednesday' and accompanied by envelope postmarked 22 June 1933, in David Garnett papers, Northwestern University.

233 Duncan Grant to Vanessa Bell, 17 May 1935 (Tate).

234 Spalding, *Duncan Grant*, p. 310.

235 Duncan Grant to Vanessa Bell, May 1936 (Tate).

236 Information from Tommy's niece Libby Goldby.

237 Ibid.

238 Julia Strachey to Frances Partridge, 15 August 1935 (King's).

239 Letter dated 8 September 1934 in Ker-Seymer papers (Tate).

240 Anne Oliver Bell (ed.), *The Diary of Virginia Woolf*, Vol. V (1984), pp. 47–8.

241   Add MS 71194, f. 177 (BL).

242   Vanessa Bell to Duncan Grant,
incorrectly dated 30 July 1930 (Tate).

243   Barbara Ker-Seymer to Rosamond
Lehmann, January 1935 (King's).

244   Theodora Gay Scott, *Cuckoo in the Powys
Nest* (2000).

245   Anne Olivier Bell (ed.), *The Diary of
Virginia Woolf*, Vol. IV (1982), entry for
6 June 1932.

246   See Hugh David, *The Fitzrovians* (1988),
Ch.8.

247   Michael Holroyd, *Augustus John*, Vol.II,
pp. 130–1.

248   Julia to Frances, 3 January 1937
(King's); David Garnett to Mina
Curtis, 2 February 1937 (Berg); *Julia*,
p. 151.

249   *Dover Express and East Kent News*,
15 January 1937, p. 10.

250   Garnett, *The Familiar Faces*, p. 176.

251   *The Times*, 16 January 1937.

252   Anne Oliver Bell (ed.), *The Diary of
Virginia Woolf*, Vol. V (Hogarth Press,
1984), pp. 47–8, quoted by kind permission of Random House Group Ltd.

253   David Pryce-Jones (ed.), *Cyril Connolly:
Journal and Memoir* (1984).

254   Alix Strachey to Eddy Sackville-West,
22 June 1937, in Sackville-West Papers
(BL).

255   Kinta Beevor, *A Tuscan Childhood* (2000),
p. 66.

256   R. F. Harrod, *The Life of John Maynard
Keynes*, p. 190.

257   Marie-Louise von Franz, *Puer Aeternus*
(2nd edn, 1981), pp. 1–2.

258   Ibid., p. 2.

259   Ibid., p. 5.

260   Ibid., pp. 8–9.

261   Ibid., p. 4.

262   Ibid., p. 8.

263   Ibid., pp. 2–3.

264   Ibid., p. 121.

BIBLIOGRAPHY

This is limited to works mentioned in the text and the notes, and does not include the extensive background literature consulted by the authors. All titles are published in London unless otherwise stated.

Ackland, Valentine, *For Sylvia: An Honest Account* (1985)

Beaton, Cecil and Buckle, Richard (ed.), *Self-Portrait with Friends: the Selected Diaries of Cecil Beaton, 1922–1974* (1982)

Kinta Beevor, *A Tuscan Childhood* (2000)

Bell, Anne Olivier (ed.), *The Diary of Virginia Woolf*, Vols. II–V (1978–84)

Bell, Quentin and others, *Charleston Past and Present* (1987)

Bell, Quentin, *Virginia Woolf: A Biography*, Vol. II (1972)

Bingham, Emily, *Irrepressible: The Jazz Age Life of Henrietta Bingham* (New York, 2015)

Bowra, C. M., *Memories, 1898–1939* (1966)

Box, Muriel, *Rebel Advocate: A Life of Gerald Gardiner* (1983)

Brenan, Gerald, *Personal Record, 1920–1972* (1975)

Brooke, Jocelyn, *The Dog at Clambercrown* (1955)

Chisholm, Anne, *Carrington's Letters: Her Art, Her Loves, Her Friendships* (2017)

Chisholm, Anne, *Frances Partridge: the Biography* (2010)

David, Hugh, *The Fitzrovians* (1988)

De-la-Noy, Michael, *Eddy: The Life of Edward Sackville-West* (1988)

Elwyn, Malcolm (ed.), *Letters of John Cowper Powys to his brother Llewellyn*, Vol. I (1975)

Franz, Marie-Louise von, *Puer Aeternus* (2nd edn, 1981)

Garnett, David, *The Familiar Faces* (1962)

Garnett, David, *The Sailor's Return* (1925)

Garnett, Oliver, *The Sculpture of Stephen Tomlin* (Cambridge disseration, 1979; copy MS in Tate Gallery Archives)

Garnett, Richard (ed.), *Sylvia & David: the Townsend-Warner/Garnett Letters* (1994)

Garnett, Richard, *Theodore Powys and the Garnetts: Record of a Friendship*, in The Powys Journal, Vol. XI (2001)

Guinness, Bryan, *Potpourri from the Thirties* (1982)

Hale, Kathleen, *A Slender Reputation* (1994)

Hamnett, Nina, *Is She a Lady?* (1955)

Harman, Claire, *Sylvia Townsend Warner: a Biography* (1989)

Harrod, R. F., *The Life of John Maynard Keynes* (1951)

Harrod, R. F., *The Prof: A Personal Memoir of Lord Cherwell* (1959)

Hastings, Selina, *Rosamond Lehmann* (2002)

Holroyd, Michael, *Augustus John: A Biography*, Vol. II (1975)

Holroyd, Michael, *Lytton Strachey: A Critical Biography*, Vol. II (1968)

Holroyd, Michael, *Lytton Strachey: The New Biography* (1994)

Hopkins, Kenneth (ed.), *The Letters of Gamel Woolsey to Llewellyn Powys, 1930-1939* (1983)

Humfrey, Belinda (ed.), *Recollections of the Powys Brothers* (1980)

Jason, Neville and Thompson-Pharaoh, Lisa, *The Sculpture of Frank Dobson* (1994)

John, Augustus, *Chiaroscuro* (1952)

Joliffe, John (ed.), *Raymond Asquith: Life and Letters* (1980)

Keynes, Richard (ed.), *Lydia and Maynard: The Letters of Lydia Lopokova and John Maynard Keynes* (1992)

Kirstein, Lincoln, *Mosaic Memoirs* (New York, 1994)

Knights, Sarah, *Bloomsbury's Outsider: A Life of David Garnett* (2015)

Lee, Hermione, *Virginia Woolf* (1996)

Medley, Robert, *Drawn from Life* (1983)

Meisel, Percy and Kendrick, Walter, *Bloomsbury-Freud: The Letters of James and Alix Strachey, 1924-5* (1986)

Meynell, Dame Alix, *Public Servant, Private Woman: An Autobiography* (1988)

Mosley, Diana, *A Life of Contrasts* (1977)

Nicolson, Nigel (ed.), *The Letters of Virginia Woolf*, Vols. III–IV (1977-8)

Olivier, Edith, *From her Journals, 1924-8* (1989)

Partridge, Frances, *Good Company: Diaries, 1967-70* (1994)

Partridge, Frances, *Memories* (1981)

Powys, Theodore, *The Left Leg* (1923)

Powys, Theodore, *The Soliloquy of a Hermit* (New York, 1916)

Pryce-Jones, David (ed.), *Cyril Connolly: Journal and Memoir* (1984)

Scott, Theodora Gay, *Cuckoo in the Powys Nest* (2000)

Spalding, Frances, *Duncan Grant* (1979)

Spalding, Frances, *Vanessa Bell* (1983)

Stinton, Judith, *Chaldon Herring: The Powys Circle in a Dorset Village* (Woodbridge, 1988)

Strachey, Julia, *Cheerful Weather for the Wedding* (1932)

Strachey, Julia and Partridge, Frances, *Julia: A Portrait of Julia Strachey* (1983)

Strachey, Lytton, *Elizabeth and Essex* (1928)

Warner, Sylvia Townsend, *A Garland of Straw* (1943)

Warner, Sylvia Townsend, *Theodore Powys and Some Friends at East Chaldon, 1922–1927* in The Powys Review, No. 5 (1979)

Woolf, Virginia, *To the Lighthouse* (1927)

Woolf, Virginia, *The Waves* (1931)

INDEX

ST = Stephen Tomlin
page numbers in italics refer to illustrations

MICHAEL BLOCH is the author or editor of some twenty works. He read law at St John's College, Cambridge and was called to the bar by the Inner Temple. During the 1980s he assisted Maître Suzanne Blum, the Paris lawyer of the Duke and Duchess of Windsor, and wrote six books about the couple. A friend of the writer and National Trust luminary James Lees-Milne, he edited five volumes of his diary and wrote his biography. His other subjects include Hitler's foreign minister Ribbentrop, the British politician Jeremy Thorpe, and F. M. Alexander, founder of the Alexander Technique. He lives in London.

SUSAN FOX is a historical researcher with special interest in the Bloomsbury Group. The authors she has assisted include Nigel Nicolson with his father's diaries and letters, Anne Chisholm with her biographies of Frances Partridge and Dora Carrington, and Laura Trevelyan with her study of her mother's family, the Winchesters. She has organised and catalogued numerous manuscript collections. She lives in the Hudson Valley near New York City with her husband and dogs.

V

At that spring I'll hold my dwelling,
Though the river flows afar;
At the spring a song's more telling
Than a moaning at the bar!

VI

For 'tis there that they would send me,
(Pray excuse the metaphor:
Play of words on 'bar' will end me
In intricacies galore!)